The Heart's Journey to Freedom

Releasing Attachment
and Finding Yourself

Jade Mazarin

The Heart's Journey to Freedom
Releasing Attachment and Finding Yourself
by Jade Mazarin

Printed in the United States of America

ISBN 9781609571405

www.xulonpress.com

PART 1: THE PROCESS OF UNDERSTANDING

PART 2: THE PROCESS OF LETTING GO

Dedication

To my father, Sanford S. Mazarin, who encouraged me to write at a young age and made this book possible.

Introduction

How many times have we known something in our heads, but felt unable to act on it? Particularly in areas like relationships, we women can feel overwhelmed by our emotions and unable to act wisely, even if we know better.

Maybe you know exactly what you would tell a friend in your situation, but it feels so different to go through it yourself. Suddenly you feel weaker than you would have expected and you just need someone to encourage you, as well as guide you in the right direction.

You have come to the right place. In this book you will find clarity and support as it relates to a certain kind of struggle—one with unhealthy emotional attachment. This includes feeling attached to the wrong person, unable to let go of a relationship that is over and/or feeling emotional about one that won't develop. Your situation can be one that has been seriously hurting you for years or one that is simply bothersome and is keeping you from a place of consistent peace.

Feeling attached to the wrong person is a very common issue that brings unrest and hardship into our lives. But while many of us don't like the way we are feeling, we might still lack the desire to let go. Others of us are sure we want to be free, but we don't know how to make that happen.

This book is meant to address those issues. I use many practical explanations and tools to help you understand attachment and find release from it. I explain why you feel what you do, how you get ready to let go and how you actually start doing it. I also complete the road by addressing the most vital part of our inner journey – our relationship with God. It is there that we find the strength to live out these principles, and there that we discover our greatest love and real identity.

I understand the nature of attachment because I have lived through it myself. I decided to write this book after I began to see my own attachment in a new light and finally decided to let it go. This altering of my approach and mindset was not something I did myself, but what God did within me. I am honored to share what I have learned with you, in hopes that I can encourage and guide you from my experience.

Thank you for joining me on this journey. You are courageous to pick up this book and seek the whole life you were intended to have. Remember that God is bigger than our weaknesses and able to inspire, to change anything, for good. May He now work His freeing power through you, as you join Him to that end.

> "Arise, shine, for your light has come,
> and the glory of the Lord rises upon you."

> (Isaiah 60:1)

PART 1

THE PROCESS OF UNDERSTANDING

Chapter 1

The Nature of Our Hearts

Inherent Power

There is nothing greater within us, nothing stronger and more dynamic, than what we truly feel. From here we live our most intense life experiences and every other area in us can flow from this mighty center. In fact, throughout the Bible the heart is used to represent not only our emotions, but also our very being. While it is the deepest part of us, it encompasses the whole person. It tends to be that if our hearts are full of something or another, the rest of our being overflows with that same thing. It can lead our behavior and experiences, our thoughts, hope and direction. We can easily follow its leading as our life unfolds.

Have you ever noticed what really drives you? Is it wisdom or logical deductions? Chances are nothing drives you quite the same way as love based emotion. That is why God desires not just rule based obedience but true, heartfelt feelings from His children. It is from the heart that our most profound motivations arise and live.

Through the heart we commune most richly with Love Himself. It enables us to enjoy Him, to follow Him and walk beside Him, in a way nothing else can. And it grants us the same capacity towards our fellow brothers and sisters. There is a truly precious nature to the awesome power of loving communion that flows from our hearts, towards our Father and His family.

As in the nature of all powerful things, God inevitably instructs us to guard our hearts carefully. Since it forms the source of our being and can affect all parts of us, it requires our careful attention.

Destined Longings

Just as the heart fills every human being with the capacity to love and live richly, there resides within each of us a strong, inexplicable desire to not only love, but to be loved. Part of being human is to long after this kind of intimate relationship. We look for deep, meaningful connections because we were made in our Creator's image; and He desires the very same thing.

In fact, even before time God has been in relationship. He has never been alone because He has always been united with His Son and Holy Spirit. Many of us are accustomed to hearing of these three figures as one being, and we are right to view them that way. At the same time, they are each separate enough to relate to one another and experience each other's company.

Just as God desires and thrives in the relationship of the Trinity, so He seeks after relationships with us - real relationships of soul full intimacy and constant communion.

Consequently, *we* have a tender, persevering desire for true intimacy. We search and long for genuine closeness, as well as united connecting. We always want this kind of loving relatedness, in the core of our being.

God's Desire to Fulfill Our Own

"Delight in the Lord and He will give you the desires of your heart." (Psalm 37:4)

The good news is that God intends to satisfy our desires. He does not build these needs within our hearts for tender interaction without meaning to address them specifically.

First, let us notice that our most fundamental needs are found with God. And they are meant to be met with Him.

When Jesus left this earth to be with His Father, He told His disciples to take heart because a great "comforter" was on His way to them. This Spirit was not only a presence to Christ's followers, but also a person to *dwell within them*. In fact, Jesus prays that He would actually be *in* His followers, just as He and God were in one another (John 17:21& 25). There is a relating, yet there is a relating so rich that it goes beyond external connecting into internal union. It is an intimacy so profound that it dispels any physical barriers, and creates continuous fellowship with God. We share with Him the most deeply intimate relationship we are able to have with anyone. We are meant to receive comfort, guidance and joy from this relationship if we are experiencing it for all it is.

However, many of us feel dry about our relationship with God, and have a stronger desire for another person to provide for our hearts. We don't yet grasp all that God can offer us. We don't seek Him with our whole heart and miss out on experiencing more of Him. We look for our joy in what we can see, and in what gives us some sort of immediate feelings of joy. Of course this tendency is not isolated to relationships. People search for a sense of happiness and meaning through money, possessions, prestige, the list goes on. Many don't even realize what they are doing or that they even have such a longing for more, until they really look within and pay close attention.

We must recognize that focusing our hope in another person or thing, despite how exciting it may initially seem, only leaves us unfulfilled in the end. We cannot focus our longing on things in this world because we weren't meant to lean on them. If we do, we will only come up empty and hurt. We will miss out on developing our inner strength and higher potential.

When we don't focus on a greater meaning than what we see, we will always want more. You see, we are designed for more. We are in fact, looking for a greater hope and a deeper kind of satisfaction.

As mentioned before, we were meant to fill this sense of longing inside us in a very specific way. We were made to first be satisfied in the deepest place within, by He who created us. No one else can fill us and address the longings that lay silently aching within us. In his book *Confessions,* St. Augustine said, "Thou hast made us for thyself, O Lord, and our hearts are restless until they find their rest in thee" (Book 1, Chapter 1).

Let us consider that the greatest of loves is found by the creator and sustainer of love itself. In fact, Scripture states that "God is love" (1 John 4:17). The remarkable thing about that verse is it speaks of God and love being of the *same substance*. It does not only say God loves. It says God *is* love.

Let us meditate upon the ever present care that falls upon us daily. It covers every part of us, richly and deeply. Yet it still overflows with more to spare. Whether we are in a place of feeling it or not, the truth of it remains. It is not altered by our ability to feel or sense it.

While the core of our being is meant to be founded in God, to make Him our first place for refreshment, we are also meant to have relational satisfaction with others. There are few things as comforting and thrilling as being refreshed by family and dear friends. We are meant to have peaceful, close-knit support from our families as a reflection of God's renewing presence. And the meaningful sharing and laughter of friends can be a tremendous gift. Again, as the Father finds joy in relationship with the Son and Holy Spirit, so we find comfort, connection and joy with our loved ones.

Thirdly, many of us are designed to find heart-felt satisfaction in marriage. Here we are meant to love deeply, work together as partners and challenge one another to live up to our given potentials in an atmosphere of care and respect.

God desires to bring together a certain son and daughter who will absolutely cherish each other and fit wonderfully together based on their unique traits. They are meant to experience true commitment and total union. Marriage is designed to be a place of great joy and comfort, as well as encouraged growth. This is the place where deep attachment is healthy and good.

The unity between a husband and wife is a beautiful thing. It is in fact, meant to symbolize the Trinity itself. Clearly marriage is a particularly special gift for God to tend to our hearts.

An Invitation

So your desires are in fact here for a reason. And they can become beautiful when brought to the right settings. But waiting in wisdom can be challenging. Even if we are in fact seeking God, even if we have decided to look only for that right person, we can still encounter temptation and confusion along the way. In fact, our journey can be downright messy! Things may seem unclear and foggy and the best paths can be hard to discover. Before we know it, we can all too easily give our deep affection to someone when it's not in our best interest. Then we just feel emotional, weaker and simply stuck.

Of course, the tricky part comes when we know we should let go, but we have a tough time being able to do it. It may seem odd to you that in some areas of your life you are strong and confidently secure. You know what you need to do and you do it. Yet in the course of relationships, you can feel utterly weak. How many times have you known you should behave a certain way, yet your feelings lead you to doing the opposite? Usually your intelligence can bring success to your life. Yet in this case, it seems toppled by the wave of emotions that periodically appear.

But God never wants His children stuck. He is now reminding us that He does indeed want more for our lives. He wants a new season full of health, inner growth and deeper joy. He wants to move us forward. He has intended for us to move forward.

God is now inviting you to let go and find your sense of peace and freedom. He is inviting you to fulfill your unique personal potential. May His Spirit speak to you about the truths of your situation and His higher plans for your future. Ladies, now is your time!

Chapter 2

What is Unhealthy Attachment?

Those who have experienced unhealthy attachment know what an up and down roller coaster it can be. Sometimes, the ride hits a plateau and we are managing reasonably well. But you never know when something is going to happen that either causes you to rise up in hope or tumble down in disappointment. The ride is tumultuous: changing unexpectedly at a fast rate or veering without notice. Our hearts are affected with each move that carries us and an internal struggle bombards us within.

....

Let's begin with the basics...what is unhealthy attachment? Unhealthy attachment, as I describe in this book, is related to being emotionally linked and unable to let go of someone that cannot or should not hold your heart. While attachment itself is any kind of emotional bond we have with others and is a natural, necessary part of life, unhealthy attachment is taking that bond into a context it should not be in. From now on when I use the term attachment, I am speaking of a certain kind of attachment that is not good for us or helpful for our well being.

Perhaps your relationship ended, but no matter how you try you can't seem to stop wanting to be with this guy or suffer from strong feelings for him. He might be leaving your life, yet he still plays a big part in your heart. On the other hand, perhaps you are friends with someone you have had feelings for, yet question if the relationship is a good idea. Maybe you both have dated at one point, maybe not. But even if you try, you have the hardest time seeing the person as simply a friend. Or take another case...maybe you have been sorely disappointed by this person's lack of attention or effort. You thought there was hope and potential for a great relationship and all you have gotten is unpredictable calls or a disinterested attitude, but you still can't seem to leave the situation alone. Then again, you might know you don't want to be with this person, but you don't see anyone else you want to be with and you are afraid to hurt his feelings. Finally, perhaps you have hung on to this relationship just barely, for too long. You realize it may not be best for you, but you don't know how to let the last bit of it go. As you can see, the scenarios of unhealthy attachment are endless!

In any of these situations you may still wonder on and off if this person really is the right one for you. Yet even if you doubt that this relationship is best for you, even if you are convinced it isn't, you can still battle with letting it go.

If you really pay attention, you will be able to connect with all or most of these symptoms of being attached...

You struggle with imagining yourself outside of a relationship with this person, despite your knowledge of what is best. You think of him too often and desire reaching out to him more than anyone else. His actions affect you more deeply, and you see him as playing an intricate part of your life. You are consistently preoccupied with what he is thinking about you and your actions, and how he will respond. You struggle with jealousy and pay close attention to his opinion of you. He inspires within you stronger emotions than anyone else and you get frustrated with yourself in the process. You want to feel secure, but continue to come back empty. The situation simply does not bring out the best in you.

Simply, when we are attached it means that on some level we have an intricate, heartfelt connection to a person, and we struggle with letting him go. No matter what difficult times we encounter, we are afraid or don't know how to change things.

Why it's unhealthy...
When you are emotionally attached to someone in the wrong context, you are in a place where total satisfaction and peaceful release cannot be found together. It is in the middle between a safe, intimate relationship and no relationship at all. It is both **unsafe and unintended.** It brings out your emotions and awakens the longings within us, but then either hurts or fails to satisfy one or both people. It tempts you with a blossomed desire for positive emotional connection, though it cannot be found there. You are in an undependable situation, with your emotions dangling on the line.

This attachment breeds **turbulent emotions** within us. We are always risking the possibility of being hurt and swayed by various circumstances that arise. Anxious feelings can nag at us to pursue or to long for pursuit. We can be nervous about how the guy will view our actions and how we can keep control. The potential for feeling angry, insignificant or jealous is always present. We do not like our behavior in such situations. On top of our anxious feelings about the situation, we feel frustrated with ourselves for allowing the battle to continue.

Sometimes staying attached can feel good. Maybe it feels familiar and safe. But the relief of giving in to what feels comfortable is mixed with an underlying sense of discomfort, fear and inner feeling of weakness. Whatever comfort we feel is minimal. It comes and goes. And therefore it is not real at all.

We feel a great deal of **confusion** when we stay attached. In the beginning of a situation we may be able to see more clearly, or if we see the relationship play out in a friend's life we can see it as it is. But once we have strong emotions rolling around in us, our eyes get foggy and we are not sure which end is up anymore. We are not sure what to do, what not to do, and what God is telling us. One day we feel we should let go, the next we aren't sure. One day we feel able, the next we feel weak. Sometimes we feel what we are doing is wrong but we don't know how to move out of it. Then our rationalizing kicks in and we think it's okay. We may even think of some good reason for it to be in our lives. Then something happens that makes us think it's not what God wants. *Back and forth. Up and down.*

There are different levels of being attached. The feeling may be so strong that nothing else is on your mind and tumultuous emotions constantly appear. Others of you, while you think about this person often, may not feel the same kind of intense attachment. The deep emotions simply come and go. The intensity of attached feelings can depend on a few things... what is going on currently (ex. continued interactions with him), the emotional dynamics of past interactions, the length of the relationship, the state of your heart at the onset of knowing him, your sense of self-esteem before and through knowing him, as well as the level of sexual intimacy the two of you shared.

It is understandable that we struggle with attachment. On the one hand, the tendency to hold on despite the cost is a true mark of commitment and love. It will be a valuable attribute in the right relationship. However, in the wrong one it is misplaced and unhealthy. It comes out distorted and sets us up for pain. It binds us to fear and apprehension. We deserve more than minimal comforts, sore emotions and stifled inner potential.

If it is so bad for us, why do we still do it?

How many times have you wondered that very question? Particularly in the moments we suffer, our minds look at what we go through and beat ourselves up over why we have allowed it. We know the hardship that can come from being attached, because we have experienced similar feelings before. Yet we still continue in the same, old patterns. Despite what we know and what others might tell us, we may not have the desire to change our habits. Then there are times when we do want to change, but we feel it is just too hard!

While each situation is unique, and you will find reasons that are attributable only to yours, here are some typical causes that prevent us from letting go...

We are comfortable with habit
We are not sure if the relationship is unhealthy
We think we might find what we are looking for here
We desire attention so deeply that parts of it are better than nothing
We minimize the pain and maximize thoughts about the good times
We can't help but think this is the only place we can find security
We have trouble understanding that we want something different
We lack deep respect and attention towards ourselves
We haven't paid enough attention to our own, independent self
We are afraid to trust God's leading and if He will guide us
We are afraid that God does not desire or have someone better for us

....

For those of you who are in a relationship and wondering if it really isn't right for you, let me explain *what a wrong relationship looks like...*

In the wrong relationship we don't feel consistent stability or a sense of inner peace. Even if we have great times, we also have very low lows. It can be dramatic and tumultuous. Perhaps you feel more insecure than you felt before, it makes you question yourself and it makes you feel like at times you can't be yourself. You have stronger emotions – sadness and/or frustration - than you ordinarily do. You feel weak and are not growing in positive ways, within. It simply feels like a lot of work. It can add stress to other areas of your life. On another note, friends or family may not approve.

Or it may just feel like something is missing. Despite the fact it looks decent logically, there is a depth and beauty missing. There is a sense of lacking that comes and goes, but keeps returning. It is a feeling deep inside that you want more, even if you can't put your finger on what more is. Something inside makes you feel like it may not be the best relationship for you.

Spiritually speaking, you may have less of an interest for God and/or feel a greater distance from Him in the wrong relationship. This is a sign that it is not a reflection of His nature or part of His plan.

On the contrary, *the right relationship* has a secure and consistently right or sincere feel to it. It doesn't need a lot of work and has a natural, steady foundation. You don't have different opinions or feelings about it from week to week. You feel like you can just be and it will all go well.

You connect with this person in a fun way, but also in a deep and meaningful one. While you will need to compromise, it will be on smaller matters for the most part and it will feel manageable. There is stability and consistent joy. You bring out good traits in each other and feel encouraged to grow personally in at atmosphere of safety and comfort. You should be able to easily make a list of all the reasons you are with this person, why he is better for you than others and why you shouldn't be with anyone else.

Finally, you feel a sense of closeness to God in the right relationship and find yourself growing in your inner potential.

....

Oftentimes in attachment we are looking for a sense of real meaning and value in our lives. We can look to this person for those things, sometimes more than we should. At times we can focus solely on him to help us feel special and lovable. Particularly when we do not consistently focus our gaze on the One who created us and created our life's purpose, we are easily tempted to look for significance and meaning elsewhere.

Looking to Control

When we are attached we tend to want control over a situation that feels out of control. We can try to build a relationship or maintain it. Or if we don't want a relationship with this person, we can still try to make each interaction a certain way, since we are sensitive to everything that takes place.

Let me begin by explaining the first example of control. Perhaps you continue to initiate talks and make moves towards this guy because you are hoping you can start a relationship or recreate one. For example, if you look for the man to ask you to get together, you might ask him if he has plans this weekend. You believe that if you do a certain thing a certain way, you can influence what he does next. Chances are the harder you work, and the more it means to you, the more attached you already feel.

Let me give you something off the bat to consider. There may be a reason even for what you don't have and what you can't get to succeed. I once had a picture in my mind when I struggled with trying to make things work. It was me pushing hard against a closed door, hoping that it would swing open. I realized there was nothing I could do to make it budge. When I pictured this, I began to wonder if it was just meant to be closed. And if that was simply the way it should be. As mentioned earlier, the right relationships are the ones that do not require continuous, draining effort that is met with minimal to moderate success.

Or perhaps you try to justify the relationship. Though you have had your concerns, you still hope beyond all hope that it can become something better. You may rationalize that it isn't that bad, other people have it worse, so why not remain with it? You wonder if this is the best that will ever come. It is sad when we are willing to accept what is "not so bad" or sometimes "just okay." In these cases we underestimate our value as well as God's intentions, since He wants to give us much more.

The second, more subtle kind of control is emotional attachment without pursuing a relationship. Here we are not trying to make a relationship happen (sometimes we may not even *want* one with him) yet we still remain feeling attached. We experience the ups and downs of emotion while we interact and our feelings are constantly on the line. We often will still try to influence the guy's behavior to make us feel good. We easily dwell on our feelings and they seem unavoidable. We may try to mentally figure out everything that is going on around us or within the guy. We may not want to upset him in any way, or we may want to upset him if we are feeling hurt.

What a burden we feel when we are attached! We start to control in an effort to feel better, thinking we can find release by making everything a certain way. The problem is we can't control every little thing. Things happen we don't want and we become tired by our efforts. In reality, we are only increasing our burden by worrying, over thinking and trying to do what we cannot.

Chapter 3

Typical Experiences

L isa had been dating her boyfriend, Jeremy, for the past two years. They had a wonderful relationship and she believed he was the man for her. True, there were many times when arguments or tension appeared between them, but he was also a great friend, and he was better than anyone she had ever expected to find. But one day in the middle of one of their fights, Jeremy told Lisa that he "couldn't do this anymore" and didn't have feelings for her like he used to. Her heart sank at the thought of what he was saying and she held her breath as tears crept into her eyes. Even though Lisa had dozens of questions in her mind...*what is wrong with me? What did I do?* She didn't have the strength to ask any of them.

It has been almost a year since that terrible night when Lisa's heart was broken. Even though the pain has lessened, she still feels deeply unhappy with herself and the situation. She dreams of Jeremy and feels a strong desire to contact him constantly. A few times the past couple months she did. But it seems he has moved on and fails to return her calls or emails. She remembers the hard times they had and knows how long ago the break up occurred. But even in her frustration she deeply misses and longs for that intimacy that they once shared. Her friends try to get her interested in other people, but deep down she only wants him. Everyone seems to feel discouraged with the situation.

....

Michelle met Steven on a Saturday night when she was out with her friends at a local restaurant. As her eyes surveyed the room looking for her waitress, she was suddenly caught off guard by the cute guy smiling right at her. Her heart skipped a beat at that moment, and the rest of the night the two continued to glance at each other and smile. When he and his friends got up to leave, Stephen came over to Michelle, introduced himself, and boldly asked for her phone number. About to burst in excitement, Michelle played it cool and casually agreed. The very next night Stephen called and Michelle couldn't believe he was that interested. They went to dinner and dancing afterwards. The chemistry was amazing. After that night they went for a walk the next weekend and another dinner a night later. It was turning out to be everything Michelle had wanted. "This is it," she said to herself, "I have finally found my man!"

A few days have passed and even though Stephen said he would call there has been, surprisingly, no word from him. Michelle occasionally looks at her phone and wishes it would ring or checks to see if there is a message she somehow missed. She keeps thinking to herself, *did I do anything wrong? I just have to know what happened.* There are countless times when she picks up the phone to call him, but then hangs up at the last minute. Last week she finally decided to leave a couple messages, but he hasn't called back. She keeps telling herself it's stupid to be so upset over a guy she was only out with a few times, no matter how much they seemed to hit it off. But the truth is that she feels hurt and angry. Despite her annoyance with Stephen, she can't seem to stop thinking about him and wonder why she couldn't finally be happy.

....

Stacy was thrilled to be in a long term relationship with such a caring, funny and intelligent man. She had many happy memories with Bill and couldn't wait to continue their future together. One day, however, Stacy's world came crashing down. She was putting a note in Bill's briefcase when suddenly a piece of paper fell from one of its pockets. As she saw it, she immediately noticed it was in a woman's handwriting. This woman made reference to their long history together and her joy about events they were now planning. She ended with, "I love you, Bill." Stacy was in shock. She looked disbelievingly at the sentimental note and felt as though she was in a nightmare. *I can't believe this. What is going on??* When confronting Bill that night, he admitted that he had been in a serious relationship for the past seven months, which was around the same amount of time he had been with her. Bill apologized for what he had done and said he was under so much stress at work that he hasn't been himself. He told Stacy she still meant a lot to him. Angry and speechless, Stacy left deeply hurt and in tears.

It has been many months since the incident, but Stacy still thinks about Bill all the time. Once in a while he will call and say he misses her. He says he wants to see her and can't imagine being without her. She asks if he has broken up with his girlfriend and he says he is going to. Stacy nervously waits, unable to think of anything else for days. When she finally hears from Bill and asks what has happened, he simply says he needs to wait. He seems to always have an excuse. He says he still wants to spend time with Stacy and she feels tempted to give in. But she knows he probably isn't good for her and tries to refrain from calling him back. Other times when he leaves heartfelt messages she feels sorry for him and returns his calls. Stacy knows she shouldn't hold on to Bill, yet she has these strong feelings that she can't shake off and they frustrate her. For some reason, she still has the desire to be with him. Sometimes it feels like it consumes her.

....

It has been two years since Eric and Emily officially became a couple. At the beginning of the relationship Eric was affectionate and attentive, but not long afterwards, he stopped going out of his way for Emily. The relationship has consisted of her calling him to get together, him being difficult to reach on the phone and her coming over to spend time at his apartment while he watches television or prepares for work. At times he even makes jokes about her weight that are hurtful to her. She has tried to talk to him about not feeling appreciated, but he says that's silly and she needs to stop being so sensitive. The more she brings up her hurt, the more she is told her feelings are not real or important. She is hurt and frustrated that he never seems to get it.

Emily has been wondering for the past year if she should break up with Eric. The problem is that she is not sure she will find anyone better. She also enjoys feeling so close to him and doesn't want to start over with anyone new. She feels very accustomed to being with him and even her disappointment has become comfortable. At least she knows what to expect. She is not even sure if she still feels in love with him and gets angry with him constantly, but it feels so much easier to let things stay the way they are. Sometimes she starts to feel the motivation to leave the relationship, but it soon fades away the moment Eric says something nice or her anger passes. She still looks for him to change (despite her many doubts) and tries to put more effort into the relationship herself, in hopes she will be treated differently.

••••••••••••••••••••••••••••••

Karen and Mike had dated on and off for almost three years. While they had plenty of drama and up and downs in their relationship, they still managed to come back as friends in between. They recently decided to work even harder on their dating relationship and lasted as a couple for five months. Though they could see it coming, they finally decided at the end of those months that they had tried all they could, and they simply were not right for each other in that way. Though it hurt both of them to admit, they agreed to only be friends from then on. But it was always difficult for them. Karen thought about distancing herself from Mike, but she was afraid of being without him and she was afraid of hurting his feelings. He was thinking the same kinds of things.

A couple months later Karen found out from a mutual friend that Mike had begun dating someone else. She felt nervous and ill as she heard this unexpected news and her response to it caught her off guard. She asked Mike about his news in their next conversation. He said that he didn't want to hurt her and that was why he didn't say anything earlier. Karen tried to sound as if she was fine, but she could only make herself sound somewhat happy for her friend. She now battles with thoughts of Mike in a relationship and struggles to see him as just her friend. She can't stop thinking about him and the situation and wonders what would have happened if they had kept trying. She can't help but constantly think about his new relationship, when he is with this girl and how she compares to her.

••••••••••••••••••••••••••••••••••••

In our lives there are countless kinds of attachment situations we can find ourselves in. There are women who start dating someone who becomes very controlling and jealous and then they don't know how to break away…..women who are married and being abused and are afraid they can't make it on their own…..women who become engaged to someone they aren't sure about, but don't know how to say no since they have been in the relationship for so long. The list goes on.

Being attached to a guy in these kinds of situations can be extremely difficult. Though the intensity of attachment varies from person to person, the feeling always creates pain in our hearts, anxious thoughts and disappointed longings. As if that wasn't enough, we proceed to beat ourselves up. *Why am I (still) feeling this way? What's wrong with me?* Maybe there are times when we think our feelings are gone. Then one little thing happens and before we know it, we are back where we started!

Sometimes our friends aren't much of a help either. They may notice our weak areas and continue to point out what we should do to change. Friends certainly mean well and want to see you happy. But sometimes their approach could be better. Perhaps while they are giving their usual advice you are saying inside, *if you only knew what this felt like!*

The Beginning of My Story

During college I met this cute, sociable guy that I was immediately drawn to. We met at a picnic lunch for freshmen and hit it off right away. We had a lot in common, great conversation and an ease that let us naturally laugh and have fun together. I felt close to him immediately, as if we had been friends for sometime already. I became even happier when I saw him taking the effort to ask me to hang out a couple more times that same weekend. I was thrilled to find such a great guy and one that seemed to feel just as interested in me.

However, as we saw each other over the next few days I noticed a progressive difference in Luke. In each day that passed, he didn't seem quite as friendly as he had been originally. I thought about him all the time and wondered if something was changing, or if it was my imagination. I remembered the great times we had and figured, well hoped, that my chances were still looking good. Of course, I needed to know that was the case. I needed to know if we were doing alright and had real hope to officially be together, or if I needed to stop hoping. I wanted to know where we stood so I could feel safe. I was too curious, too impatient and wanted it to work too much, to wait. I also wanted to show him that I was in fact interested. You know, in case he didn't know already and was holding back for my sake.

So one night I bit the bullet. I nervously asked him how he saw me and what was going on between us. He replied by saying that he liked me very much as a friend, but that he didn't want to start dating anyone right now. Ouch. I felt rejected and let down. But I took a breath. I told him calmly as if completely unaffected, that that was fine and I understood it completely. Huh…right. *Yea, I didn't want you either!*

Over the next month, I felt awkward around Luke and I had always hated that feeling more than anything. I tried to pretend everything was fine, as did he, but I did not feel comfortable or close to my new friend and I missed that. I would try to talk to him and make things comfortable between us, but it still felt strange. I was saddened that it had to end this way and I was mad at myself for bringing up the infamous, "let's define this" conversation.

Over the next few weeks however, our situation began to change. Luke and I were thrown into a couple social events together and we began to find a way to tease one another and find comfort again. Our friendship grew quickly from there and we became very close. Over the course of many months,

Luke and I spent a great deal of time together. I still had feelings for him, but I tried to keep them to myself. Of course part of me never stopped hoping that maybe he felt the same way and now wanted to be with me.

There were moments we spent time together when he was especially attentive and easily flirtatious. After these times I only liked him more and then couldn't help but ask how he felt about me, hoping his feelings had changed. But he said he only wanted to be friends. Other times he said he was interested in dating me, but feels he it wouldn't be a good idea (whatever that meant). Boy did that frustrate me. One night, he told me he wanted to go on an official date with me. Of course I was thrilled. I expected that after that night we would be "dating," but he started to pull back again. Once again I couldn't help but pursue another talk with him (yea, I really didn't know when to give up!) only to hear he had changed his mind. I couldn't help but feel as though I was never good enough.

This feeling of inadequacy only got worse when I heard about a girl that Luke was interested in. I wondered why he liked that girl and not me. Or why he wanted to be with her and not me. I hated the thought of him being in a relationship with someone else. Even when I tried to treat him as a platonic friend, I felt like I was walking on a tight rope when Luke would mention someone. I didn't know what he would say next and I would almost hold my breath in apprehension. My footing at these times shook with each step on the bouncing, thin wire. Instead, I wanted so often to feel a steady, large and solid ground beneath me. One in which I didn't need to be afraid of what he would say or what would happen with him. I would still be secure.

The place in which we find ourselves when we are attached is undependable. Our emotions are constantly on the line and we do not know what will occur today or tomorrow, to let them loose in a certain direction. We don't feel good about ourselves, we are scared about what will happen next and we don't feel good about how we are behaving.

When you are attached to someone in the wrong situation, it is an all lose situation. Whether or not you desire to be "with" him your feelings still arise. They distract you and tempt your faith away from what could be better. Good times are not really good because they increase your desire for someone you cannot or should not be with. And you are drawn into a distressing situation that cannot satisfy. Of course bad times are not that much better, because you feel the stinging pain of negative interactions and hurtful let downs.

God does not desire for his children to be in an incomplete, difficult middle point. He does not desire our needless heartache or possible suffering. He wants his children to be safe and fulfilled. If a place is not designed to satisfy completely our heart's longing, then He desires us to have total peace. And attachment to the wrong person, or in the wrong situation, is neither fulfilling nor peaceful.

Focusing on the Guy

When we are attached to someone it can be difficult to not focus on him at some level or another. In fact, sometimes it seems impossible. Recent interactions with this person float through your mind at random points throughout the day, bringing along familiar feelings that touch your heart or make you angry. You desire for him to act a certain way or do a certain thing. You run it through your mind often. Some of your thoughts create frustration and concern. Just like most thoughts about him, they easily draw you into questioning and dwelling. You think about the topics you and he have covered or you focus on what's occurring in his life. Your thoughts about him, the different directions they take, and the emotions they stir within you, feel automatic. Phew! This flood of thoughts can be plain tiring!

Then again, there are times your preoccupation with this person is intentional. Maybe you think you can figure something out…make sense out of him or why you feel the way we do. You may try to prepare yourself for what you know is coming, even if it scares you. For example, if you know this person has started to date someone else, you imagine it so that you can get used to the idea, in hopes you can let him go. Usually, however, such thoughts come at very unwanted times with unwanted hurt. When you are emotionally attached, whatever makes you jealous has a terrible tendency to sink in your mind uninvited.

When we are attached to someone, everything they do affects us. While we may not be very bothered by a friend's comments in a given conversation, the same words create much stronger feelings within us if they were made by the person we are emotional about. All the same, you never know when something could be said that is exactly what you wanted to hear. And in this case, what is said feels better than if anyone else in the world said it to you. Suffice it to say, everything this person says and does holds a significance and power that is exclusive to him.

If most of what this guy does holds importance, than so does what might be underneath. We females are infamous for analyzing an occurrence to death, or for considering the possible, deeper meaning in everyday interactions. The more we feel for this person, the more we feel it is necessary and automatic to do this. When this guy says something we may wonder why he said it. Or we may assume we know why he said it, and then experience either joy or unhappiness. It seems that whatever reasons or motivations drive this guy, they are as important to us as what they drive him to do.

Looking for Something

As we have established, there are probably things you have wanted this person to do or not do. Whether he is making us furious or "just" getting on our nerves, these feelings come because he is failing to give us what we look for. We may be hoping for a genuine apology or change of action. We may want real listening and a display of care. If we don't get these things, it can raise our annoyance or lower our spirits. After all, *we* would respond to someone in that certain manner, wouldn't we? Because our emotions are there, it is hard not to want these comforts from this person.

Unfortunately, when we do not receive signs that we are cared about, we can only want them more, and feel driven to seek them more directly.

Let's take a simple example. Say this person hasn't called you back and it makes you concerned. You start to wonder and hope, that maybe he didn't get your message (though you don't see why he wouldn't). Mostly, you want to hear him validate that you are important. So you ask, "I called last week...did you get my message?" He pauses and then says, "Yea, I did," but nothing else. You think to yourself, *is that all you're going to say?* You hope he will have a good reason for failing to call back since you don't want to think he avoided you or didn't want to talk. You're also a bit annoyed that he didn't elaborate. Now you feel more emotional about the whole thing and feel like you can't just let it go. You can't help but say, "Sooo...why didn't you call me back?" At this he begins getting annoyed and says, "(silence)...I didn't have time." This response of course, only makes you feel more nervous, annoyed and hurt that he doesn't seem to care.

Now you feel worse both because of his reactions as well as your sensitivity to them. It is almost as if you can see yourself from an outsider's perspective and you don't like what you see. This dilemma is familiar to you, yet it still occurs.

This same scenario can be applied to many different conversations. The point is that they can easily follow a sequence of us saying/doing something to get the response we are looking for and then our continuing to do it (now out of more frustration) because we now need it more. Our efforts in getting what we want have blown up in our face. The more we try to get what we want, the more hurt we feel when it doesn't happen. Then we feel even more desperate.

As we can see, the search for affirmation and safety is a vicious cycle that feeds upon itself.

Reflecting Back on Us

A large reason this man's relating to us is so significant is it affects the way we see ourselves. We feel that if we have his respect and admiration, we have more of our own. At what level this happens is determined by the strength of the attachment and the way of seeing ourselves before and through knowing the guy.

The reason we desire certain words from him, moments of affirmation and particular displays of care, is because through them we receive messages that we are worth it and we are safe. We are beautiful, appealing and special. We then feel good about ourselves because we put a lot of emphasis on this person's opinion when we are emotionally attached to him. The problem is that by giving this guy the responsibility to ascribe (even in its smallest amount) any kind of worth to us, we are giving authority over to someone who is not meant to have it.

But let's now take a different example. Say you are close to a guy who you don't want a relationship with, but you enjoy spending time with him and you have some feelings for him. One day he gets preoccupied with work and doesn't call you as he often does. Perhaps it takes days for him to get back to you. Suddenly, you are feeling things you haven't felt before. All the feelings you had, and the insecurities you didn't even know were in you, are rising to the surface. You are completely afraid he is ignoring you, no longer wants to talk to you or even could have met someone else. You start to feel less cared about and less important. You are worried you have done something wrong and can't wait for him to call you in hopes that you haven't. You want to feel safe, good about yourself, and see that you haven't hurt his feelings so you don't have to feel guilty. All of these things you are looking for from this guy. You want to know everything is okay between you and you want to know that you are valuable because you are still important to him.

Let's also be aware that this pattern can happen outside of our current situation as well. We may have given up on finding the care we look for from this particular guy and instead we are looking for it from other guys. The hurt we experience travels with us if we do not address it and learn to grow our sense of self-worth another way.

Where Our Value Really Comes From

The truth is that God is the only path to a deep sense of value and inner strength. We must remember that God is a Person to deeply connect with, just as we connect with those we see. He is not some intangible substance and He is just as real as what is in front of us. He has real feelings, real thoughts. He has a dynamic, constant love for us that makes Him long to hear our voice or see us looking for Him. He views us as beautiful brides and thirsts for our heart attention, though we may give it to others. He hangs on our every word and is constantly thinking of even our smallest thoughts or daily events. And anything important to you is important to God. He says, you are **"My treasured possession** (Exodus 19:5)....*and I rejoice over you with singing"* (Zephaniah 3:17).

It is only His love that has the power and authority to ascribe value to us. We may feel this guy is valuable and his thoughts matter, but he comes no where near the value and substance of God, and what His love says about us. It is God alone who grants us importance, and one we can count on.

There is also an inherent value to us because we are daughters of a King - the Creator and Lord of the earth. Those who are royalty are supposed to be treated with respect simply because of where they come from.

Only God created us and really knows us inside and out, so only He can give us an accurate account of who we are. Other people are not equipped in enough wisdom and clarity. They have their own issues and blind spots and can easily diverge from the truth. They also do not have the power to give beauty to us or to take any of it away. It is just not about another person's opinion (which we often only guess about, anyway).

Even if every person gave you the validation you want, there would come a point in time when even that wouldn't feel like enough. Once again, our hearts are restless until they find rest in God.

Being in Touch with Internal Experiences

What about the particular situation you may be dealing with...how has it changed or stayed the same to you? How would you want things to be different? Before we address even the possibility for change we have to know what could use changing.

There are of course times when we do not want to face our situations. There is a part of us that sees what we are doing and is ashamed of it. Because of these uncomfortable feelings, we might try to pretend it is not a big deal and/or we will purposely ignore what is going on.

There have been many times when I tried not to pay attention to a subtle voice in me that told me what I was doing wasn't right. Not that I didn't hear it, but I simply didn't want to listen. It came particularly when pursuing time with a guy I should be letting go of...*you know you shouldn't be doing this, Jade.* However, instead of allowing this thought to change my behavior, I would try to block it out. I didn't want to hear if I was doing something unhealthy. That would mean I would have to either stop doing it (something I really didn't want to do) or feel bad about myself the whole time I did. Who wants that?

There are also times we have a negative opinion of our behavior and listen to it, but make ourselves feel better by rationalizing. For example, how many times have we gone out of our way for a guy and pretended it was no big deal? "This is just something I do for my friends," you might say. Something in you may know more, but you allow reasoning to drown it out. That can be an easy thing for us to do.

We can always find a way to reduce the volume of the opposing voice. The problem is that no matter how we do it, the things we do that continue attachment still hurt us. They keep the habit going and they keep us feeling stuck.

Likewise, through these moments we develop an opinion of ourselves. If we are doing something that feels weak or unhealthy, then something in us says we are weak or unhealthy. Even by drowning it out with reasoning, the lingering whisper will not go away. This only sets us up for not having strength in future choices as well.

Our feelings about ourselves in these times are like warning signals that tell us we are acting against our potential and need to stop. Instead of trying to ignore what our sense is telling us deep down, we need to not only pay attention to it, but also fine tune its discernment. When questioning the validity of these thoughts, we need to ask God for clarity and wisdom. If operating from His insight, our inner feelings can tell us what is going on and they can be a great guiding system. They are for our good. And we need to no longer be afraid of what is good for us.

It is important that you be honest with yourself. Let yourself consider if what you are doing is healthy or not. Consider if the action leaves you feeling good and strong, or sad and weak. This will shed some light on what could use changing. Allow yourself to face the truth. Don't be ashamed of it because chances are, your thoughts or behavior are common and understandable. So notice they are there. Even if you haven't decided yet if you are going to loosen your grip, at least notice the struggle within you. Then don't be afraid to consider letting go of what keeps you stuck. God is always inviting you to more, waiting for you to take Him up on it. Amidst the difficulty, He can make it feel easier and more possible when we choose to begin letting Him.

Honesty with God

As you are noticing how you feel and behave, you can take the time to share with your Father. How funny it is to me that sometimes we don't express what we are thinking to God and assume He may just not notice what we are hiding. The truth is He knows very clearly everything that goes through your mind. In fact, He knew what you would be thinking about even before you were thinking about it! It is senseless for us to hide anything we feel or do from Him.

So we have established that God knows everything. But that may not even be a strong enough case for us to share our struggles with Him. I think this one is...He *empathizes* with you. He empathizes with every part of you. Every load of weakness, every tinge of struggling sin, none of it goes unloved or unappreciated. God feels deeply for the heart of his daughters. There is nothing you have experienced or are experiencing that God does not recognize completely, or understand fully. No one can empathize more.

Now let me add something you may not have considered. God not only feels for what you are going through, He actually *feels* it Himself. God actually feels what you are feeling because His Spirit lives in you. What an incredible thought! The God of the World...this Huge, Mighty Lord, is also so intimate with His little children that the essence, the "personhood" of God lives in them. Therefore, He experiences what you do. How often can you say that about someone else in our life? Even your closest, most dear friend, cannot feel your emotions exactly the way you do. Wouldn't it be wonderful to have that kind of deep understanding from someone? How about with Someone who also knows what you've come through *and how you can feel better?*

Through sharing your thoughts with God you are both deepening your relationship with your greatest love and help, as well as practicing real honesty with yourself. You are allowing yourself to face the things you may be trying to ignore. You can learn how to be more aware of what you are doing, and less afraid to face it in its entirety. You can then know where you are right now, in order to see where you need to be going.

May you share with God by praying to Him with honesty. You can be totally vulnerable because He is safe and understanding. Sharing with God is not like opening up to some Originator of the Universe. It is receiving the comforting communion with the Lover of your Soul. It is reaching out to a perfect Father who sees what you are going through and experiences it with you. He doesn't judge you for the times you falter, or how long it has taken you to let go. He only has compassion for you. Though it brings sorrow to His heart to see you hurting or limiting yourself, He can see the reasons behind your feelings or behavior. And His heart is moved by yours. All the while He *never* stops seeing the potential in you towards freedom and greater strength that you didn't know was possible.

By sharing your thoughts and feelings with God, you can be touched in the deepest, most needed place in your heart. Remember that no matter how long you have struggled, no matter how many ups and downs you face, God is always patient. He loves you just as much as if you never had this (or any other event, no matter what it is) in your life. Nothing influences His unchanging love for you or His pleasure in who you are. Allow yourself to be seen and learn that everything you have to present is alright. You can learn that it is safe to admit your thoughts and feelings because if God does not judge you for them, it is not necessary to judge yourself either.

You perceive my thoughts from afar,
You discern my going out and my lying down;
you are familiar with all my ways.
Before a word is on my tongue
you know it completely, O Lord.

(Psalm 139:1)

Chapter 4

What You Really Want

While we are on the roller coaster of attachment, there are plenty of moments that make us feel ill. Part of us hates it, but there is another part that can't seem to get off at the stops breezing past. We have to want to leave it enough to make the jump and we keep on hesitating. Why do we do this? It is the battle between what we think we want and what we really do. And attending to the smallest desire to hold on is influential enough to keep us trapped.

....

What You Want

Oftentimes we can be upset with ourselves for not being able to let go and we wonder why nothing we do seems to be working. Perhaps you have wanted to let go for sometime and you've been trying your best. *So why do I still feel this way?* You ask in frustration. There is a reason we don't get out of the cycle. And that is this....we haven't decided if we *really* want to. It's true. If letting go was what you wanted the most, you would just do it. There is a reason you want to hang on, despite the hurt it causes. There is always a reason for the things we do. So why would you want to continue this? Because even if it causes you pain, there are times it gives you what you look for.

We have already established that we all want to feel cared for and significant. We want attention and affirmation. And we may want this guy because there is a chance he can give that to us, even in a small amount. What about those memories you have of joyful times together, or the hope that those would surely come? There may be plenty of fun and loving times you have shared with this person. Even if they may have lessened they can always return, right?

While in many cases we may not even get the intimate attention we look for, we may get it in some fashion and think that is better than nothing at all. We may get it in pieces and don't want to lose what little we have. Or we may hang on in hopes that more will appear or will finally stay for good.

We think that if we let go, we avoid the chance to finally receive what we have longed for. If we let go, this really won't work out. By hanging on we leave open the *possibility* for more joy in the future.

It could be that remaining attached keeps the door at least cracked open with this relationship. That bit of hope can be relieving or comforting. It also could be that you are simply lonely. Or that you feel you need this person to give your life greater meaning or to give yourself a sense of importance. You may not know how to define yourself as your own person. You may not know how to see yourself apart from this man since you have been with him (or someone else) for so long.

As mentioned earlier, many of us remain attached simply because we are used to it. Experiencing what we are used to gives us some sense of comforting security. Likewise, after some time the feeling is so common that being without it feels empty and frightening. You are accustomed to its presence in your heart. And strangely, even the anxiety it can create feels both disturbing and comfortable at the same time.

The point is that we continue doing something unhealthy for us because we are getting some sort of a payback from it. There is something that makes us feel good about holding on. And if what we are getting (even in its small amount) is overly important to us, then we won't choose freedom.

Misplaced Longings

Sometimes we are looking for what was lacking in a significant relationship many years ago. Your desire for love or any other heartfelt experience may feel remarkably deep and desperate, because it has been starved for a love that was missing for sometime. Now you may be looking for it in the wrong places. You may look for any chance to get it. Maybe you have not experienced love or known what being really cared for feels like, and you can't seem to strip yourself away from what seems like the possibility to have it. Maybe you have always been looking to fill this void and you jump at any opportunity to feel complete. It seems impossible sometimes, to walk away from the chance at love; particularly, if this guy has shown you moments of care and thoughtfulness.

On the other hand, you may have tried to fiercely ignore your desires in order to avoid possible pain or vulnerability. You have built up a wall for your own feeling of protection. You question the safety of acknowledged feelings or the trustworthiness of other people. After all, many people have let you down in your life. It is just not safe to give your heart to someone. Remaining attached gives you some intimacy, while not getting your hopes up, since there is only so much you know you'll get in return. There is a strange "safety" in knowing where you stand and that it will not disappoint you since its limitations are clear.

Think about your past relationships. In particular, I would like to call first your attention to childhood memories with your parents. Did you receive unconditional, constant love from them? Did you feel special and valuable to them? On the other hand, did you feel overly tended to by them so that you had trouble finding independence? The way we were treated by our parents and how we felt about ourselves as a result, can influence us greatly in our future relationships.

Now let's jump to your friend and dating relationships while growing up. Do you notice any patterns? Any kind of pain that we have experienced in those early relationships can create within us fear and unfulfilled needs. Any kind of message we received about dependency on others, or lack of individuality, can affect us as well.

Many of us do not consider how we were treated as children and adolescents as connected to our present life. But in actuality, this is one of the most significant times for learning about ourselves and relating to other people. It is a time that can shape our opinions long into the future. A childhood that was void of consistent acceptance and loving attention can influence us to desperately look for those things in future relationships. At the same time, a parental relationship that was too constricting, where nothing could be done apart from others, can also influence us to behave in unhealthy ways. Here we can feel we need extreme intimacy and we are lost without it.

If you can see negative patterns in your relationship life or ways of thinking that you or others see as unhealthy, I strongly recommend you to consider counseling. Doing an honest evaluation of ourselves, getting into our core wounds and seeking help, is one of the wisest, most courageous and important things we can do. It frees us up to greater potential for joy and peace the rest of our lives. In fact, most of us could use counseling at one time or another. We need not do this alone, and oftentimes we shouldn't.

While we can't ignore the influence of the past on our present, we also must realize that this is a different time and we *can* achieve real freedom today. We are never bound by the past. We always have the choice to take whatever route we want to from here. We have come to a new time in our lives. And now it is up to us.

Trying to Get our Desires Met – Once Again

Right now I would like to expand upon the habit to influence this guy to do what we want in order to feel cared for and safe.

Let me give you another example. When dating a man, you may notice he is pulling back. After waiting and getting nothing new, you take matters into your own hands and make happen what you have waited for. You initiate time with him, talks with him and moments that increase your sense of intimacy and closeness. Maybe you have done this many times in the past, while the guy rarely reaches out to you, yet you cannot quite give up. In fact, you are willing to risk your own sense of respect for the slim chance of feeling special and experiencing the tender love that could be there. Your desires are so strong that you feel walking away is too scary. It would mean that you have to remain with your feelings of being unloved and give up on the precious *chance* for something more.

Though we think our efforts will improve the relationship, they usually backfire. Maybe the moments are not as satisfying as you expected. Maybe the guy begins feeling suffocated or tired of your continuous initiating. And quite possibly, you are losing more of an internal sense of your value and identity, while receiving little or none of it back from the man you look to. You feel weaker and less confident in yourself. Whatever positive response you may get is small, unpredictable and inconsistent. Before long you are back where you started. Internally you continue feeling that you need someone to raise you up, because now you feel lower than ever.

Even if you are not pursuing the desire to make the time with this guy, you can still be mentally obsessing over what is going on. You may be in despair that he is not reaching out to you as you wished, while you may be afraid to reach out to him yourself. But you just keep wishing he would act differently and you simply can't stop hoping something will change.

In these situations, we can be looking to fulfill a natural desire for love and attention. But we can also be looking to fulfill a deeper longing that was left unfulfilled most of our lives. It is useful for us to consider if there would be a cause for needier searching and if a greater void is missing. Or if we are simply letting our emotions lead us in the wrong direction because they can.

Then there are times we are just trying to meet our desire for companionship. The reason for holding on is plain…we just don't want to be lonely. It is easy to assume that what we have now is better than having nothing at all. I completely understand that. I know what it is like to have someone to spend time with and not want to be on alone.

The Truth of the Matter

While you derive some benefit from holding on, there is much distress that goes along with it. So much in fact, that it takes over any good thing that you're getting.

As you approach letting go, you must realize a few things…First, **the benefits are not enough.** They are some forms of attention, some joy in companionship, but you desire more and can't have it, especially on a consistent basis. This middle place does not satisfy you, but only drives you to deeper emotions, which causes more future turmoil.

Your pleasant memories and what you take from them may also be merely selective and there is a much bigger picture to consider. Secondly, **the benefits are couched in negative experiences.** They bring you sadness and/or anger and they can be unpredictable. Thirdly, while you look for this guy to make you feel better about yourself, **you feel even worse about yourself.** You are not getting the sense of security, inner strength and feeling of value that you look for. What he offers is not enough. Lastly, this attachment **keeps you from better things.** This situation can close the door to things like - gaining a deeper self worth by learning how to find it in yourself, uncovering meaning and companionship with God, and finding the right relationship.

You must face and own the fact that the negative outcomes of attachment far outweigh the positive ones. That being said, *what do you really want?*

What You Really Want

Of course we have all experienced more than once the desire to remain attached, while simultaneously wanting to let go. You may truly enjoy feeling as though you are with this person. But your mind fights your heart and critiques you as foolish or unwise. You may have times when you feel placed on a pedestal and others when you are thrown down without notice. We have established so far, that there will always be times of certain joy mixed unpredictably with aching pain or pesky anxiety.

That being said, I have something to ask you…after an honest, realistic assessment of your current situation, "What do you want?" No, think about this way… "What do you *really* want?" That is the key here. Not what we might think we do, but what we really do. In order to answer this question, we have to be aware of ourselves and of what we need.

Sometimes we may think we want a particular person, when what we really want is love. So if we are unable to get it from this man, do we still want to be with him? I don't think so. We think we want to be, but by being with this person we do not get what we are looking for. Therefore, deep down we do not want this person if he cannot offer us our sought after gift: love.

Similarly, do you want sudden pain or continued nagging worry? Do you want to feel poorly about yourself in frustration? If you know this is the pattern, what makes you think it will change? Once you truly believe things are what they are, you will see the only reason to hold on is for more pain. Alright, so you get some desires met. Now, let me say I do not mean to underestimate the immense power of that, truly. But let us remind ourselves of what we already wonder about…much of what we do receive in attachment is burdensome, heavy and robs us of our feeling of self satisfaction. There isn't much good (if any) in it. If we live in constant apprehension that any positive change will soon leave, we are not joyful, even in those nice times. Can't life be peaceful and feel good? Yes, outside of attachment. So what do you think… what do you really want?

You are in a no win situation while you are attached. On the one hand, the man upsetting you creates your sadness and frustration. One the other hand, his impressing you encourages your attachment to something that cannot and should not be yours - something that will inevitably let you down.

What I often didn't realize, was that I wanted more than the guy. I wanted more than certain actions from him. Instead, I wanted something greater than that. I wanted my own sense of rest, my own feeling of strength and independence. While being attached, I didn't feel good about myself and I didn't enjoy the experience. I wanted to think about him and not feel burdened by the need to dwell. Hear him say something and not be fueled in frustration. I wanted to relax my focus on him and not worry, not care so much. In short, I wanted freedom. I wanted to be able to breathe. And I wanted to feel confident, not weak or insecure. Anytime we are attached to another person, what we actually want more is freedom. That is because our souls were designed to want health. The question is whether or not we realize we want peace more than the rest of it. When we listen to our deepest needs our desires flow naturally towards true freedom and joy.

Lining up with God

"Direct me in the path of your commands, for there I find delight." (Psalm 119:35)

I am going to go out on a limb for a moment and say that I believe most of the time what we really want is also what God wants for us. *Wait a minute, is that possible?* You might wonder. Of course there have been plenty of times when we have wanted something God has not wanted for us. But we are also shortsighted, emotional and unable to see the whole picture, as God can. Our human selves grasp for the upper hand and seek out what we momentarily desire, but not most deeply. And not in the long run. If we did not have these distracting limitations, I wonder how our desires might be different.

Let me explain further. First of all, God always wants what is best for us. He wants a situation that will bless and grow us. He wants something in our lives that will bring us joy and move us towards our potential. Do we not want the same thing? If you had multiple situations in front of you and the results of each one could be seen at the same time, would you not choose the one that came out best? We all desire the greatest freedom, love and sense of contentment we can receive. The reason we fail to go after these things at times is not because we do not desire them, but because *we misunderstand where they are found.* Based on our emotions and shortsightedness, we become confused or careless. We do desire the right things, but we may not know where to find them.

Secondly, we want right things because God's Spirit lives in us. Christ has taken the weaker, stained parts of us and freely given us His character and newness. He has also given us the gift of the Holy Spirit to dwell within our being. This new self forms our deepest identity as His followers. This being said, the depth of us consists of God's Spirit and desires what is good and true. Beneath the noise of our confusion and emotions, there is a quieter, greater core that wants the kinds of things that God wants for us. Sometimes we just have to start looking for it and paying attention to it. Then it will become clearer. It is just a question of looking beneath the noise of our emotions and confusing thoughts, and sensitively paying attention to a richer, more peaceful sense within.

Chapter 5

Surrendering to God
A Deeper Spiritual Look

Before the Fall we were closely knit to our beloved Lord. Adam and Eve communed with God the way that one would spend time with a dear friend. They talked, and smiled I am sure, always enjoying each other's company. Everything was right because God was in complete control. As the Creator, God had the earth and all that was in it under the shield of His good will, where there was safety and freedom. After some time, however, the state of the world changed forever. People became different, as they no longer regarded their God. They forgot His love and constant providence. They decided to try and take His place, as if they did not need Him.

As a precursor to eating fruit from the Tree, Eve had a decision to make. Was she going to listen to God and hold back because He told her to? Was she going to trust His wisdom and respect His authority? Or was she going to doubt if His leading was in her best interest and take matters into her own hands? Well, we know what happened. Though God had led her in a particular direction, Eve was deceived into believing that maybe His ways were not intended for her good and she needed to be in charge. She decided to override God's instruction and to act like god of her own life.

Often we are tempted to do the same thing. We are faced with a situation and are unsure if God has enough interest or investment in our happiness to lead us in the right direction. Sometimes, we are not even sure if that direction will be made known to us. We wonder if God will take the time out from His more important schedule to guide our personal lives. We are simply afraid. So we take control of it ourselves. And finally, let's face it…we also struggle with loving our desires more than we love God. So we do whatever we can to get what we want most.

The problem is, we were not designed to be self-sufficient, nor were we designed to worship any other thing besides God. So when we do what we were not created to do, we can easily get lost.

You can see from my earlier story that I always tried to make things work as I was growing up. After all, if you want something to happen you just have to do it yourself. I put all the responsibility for success on myself. I followed my emotions because they called my attention. I thought if I followed their lead, I'd be happy. Though I knew God and cared for Him, I wasn't aware of how that related to this area of my life. I didn't know about God's capable level of involvement, His desire to make me happy and the fact that He really did know best. I wasn't aware that He was safe to surrender to and had the power to bring good things all on His own.

However, despite my avid efforts to control, my plans always failed in the end. Instead of finding happiness, I was often left with was sore disappointment, nagging worry and the heavy burden of wondering how I could still fix things. I'd replay events in my mind and wonder about what I could have done to make them better.

As if seeing my behavior from an outsider's perspective, I wasn't proud of myself. I knew my actions and thoughts were overly emotional, weak and afraid. I didn't respect the person I saw. I hoped and prayed that I would change one day. Of course, I didn't know what I as in for when I asked for that.

My Pivotal Moment of Faith

It was springtime, and Luke actually decided he wanted a serious relationship with me. Yes, you heard me. Surprised? So was I. *I cannot believe this is happening!* I thought to myself. Of course I was simply thrilled…the moment had come. Yet oddly enough, I also felt something else. It was a subtle feeling that I had other times in the year, but had ignored. Now it seemed to reappear, annoyingly. It was some sort of gut-level feeling that a romantic relationship with Luke was not best for me. In fact, it even felt as if was God asking me to not go forward. I couldn't understand, since Luke and I had great times together and he was also close to God. I saw some clashing differences in us, but they were easy to gloss over. In any case, my bothersome feeling was now showing up again. I even had a mutual friend confirm to me – though I had said nothing to him – that he didn't feel it was right.

Before I go on, I would like to explain this feeling I had. I didn't have much of a case for it logically speaking. Luke was a great friend and good person. Our differences were more irritating than problematic. I didn't care about them. After all, I had an enormous crush on him! There seemed no logical reason for me to feel a lack of peace, a sense of unrest, about going forward. But I had these feelings in a place that went deeper than my emotions. Beneath my loud, distracting feelings was a different kind of feeling. It was more of a knowing. It was a sense. It was quiet but steady. It came from God's Spirit which was in me.

As I considered that God was asking me to let go, I became angry, sad and scared. This kind of thing never worked for me. And now that I finally have what I wanted *He is going to take it away?* It was painful to imagine saying "no" to something I had wanted more than anything. So painful in fact, that I knew I was battling with more than this situation. I was confronting old, ingrained ways of living that had consumed my heart for years. I was confronting fears of being out of control, distrust in God to act and want my joy, and pain to let go of what I wanted for Someone I couldn't see. I felt the fear and weight of changing a deep place in my heart.

The truth is I never surrendered to God not only because I didn't really trust Him, but also because He wasn't the most important thing to me. As a Christian who was taught to prioritize God, I would have liked to say He was first in my heart. But when you look at the evidence of how I lived, you could tell I put my wants above seeking what He wanted. I surrendered to my desire and to other guys, rather than surrendering to God and what He wanted. *And whatever we surrender to is what's really most important to us.*

They say God works in mysterious ways. This event was not just about dating Luke. God didn't care about my dating someone as much as He cared about becoming the leader of my life and the priority of my heart. So in His vast creativity, God used this event to give me an opportunity. He was inviting me to surrender to Him. He was asking me to trust Him enough to let go and to love Him enough to follow His lead. The hardest part, was I knew it was up to me – He was giving me the choice. It was a huge decision, and it felt extremely heavy (I now understand it felt this burdensome because it was a pivotal moment that would change my life forever).

I spent much time in honest prayer, even venting my frustration with God. I told Him I was angry that He wanted to take this away from me and doesn't He want my happiness? I told Him I was scared I wasn't hearing from Him and to please make it known if I was making this up. I told Him I didn't know if I could do this. I knew He was my father and that He could take the honesty. I experienced gut-wrenching tears and countless times of prayer. I was very afraid of taking this leap of faith. It felt so different from anything I had ever done and again, what if I was wrong?! I went back and forth, wondering if He really was asking it of me. But the feeling kept returning. I then dared to believe that He would set me straight if He needed to.

Over the next few days though still afraid, I felt some strength come into me. I also felt I couldn't push away what I had been feeling. I simply knew I couldn't walk away from my Father. Somewhere inside I also felt that I must have been asked to not proceed for my own good. Though it was easy to doubt His desire to bring me joy, I knew there must be more to this than I understood. Knowing God, His request had to be for my protection.

I began to learn then how to conquer that great, human challenge of surrendering control. I learned what it meant to take a great step for God, daring to trust that He is kind, wise and completely able to be my guide. I began to understand what it's like to love God most and to make Him the most important thing in my life.

Then one night I was sitting on my porch with my Bible open on my lap. I told God that I was sorry for putting guys above Him all my life. I told Him that I would now make Him the most important thing to me. Just then, a breeze swept over the book. It picked up a corner of the page I was on and held it up, thereby revealing a passage on the next page. This passage was Isaiah 42:8-9. I looked down and read...

"I will not give my glory to another, nor my praise to idols. See, the former things have taken place, and new things I

declare; before they spring into being I announce them to you."

Pretty amazing, don't you think? I smiled and looked up at God. I thanked Him dearly for showing me that He really *was* with me.

This experience was not only a turning point in my faith, but also in me. Through my surrendering I felt stronger and more secure. Through greater closeness to God, I felt more of His peaceful power in my heart. *Though I seemed to have given up what I wanted, I actually gained what I had been looking for.* I began to feel more at peace, as things were no longer dependent on me. I didn't need to worry or manipulate because I wasn't the one who could make the right things happen.

I began to learn that my meaning and sense of self came from Someone greater than guys. Although I always tried to tell myself that, now I actually *felt* it. It was a surprising result of becoming closer to God – feeling different on the inside. My heart started changing and I felt a worth on my own. For the first time I didn't feel a need for a boyfriend. I also saw the blessing of past relationships that failed to work. I began to feel very strongly that a wonderful relationship would be given to me one day. I knew it would be the kind I always hoped for. And I knew God would be the one to bring it.

How this story applies....
Many women find themselves in the same situation I was in. They may not like to face it, but in reality they put guys and their desires, above their love for God. Many women also deal with being afraid to trust Him (as I had said earlier) and feeling the nagging need to act themselves.

I share this story because unhealthy attachment can be a symptom, and I am after the place it comes from. I want to address this deeper place that impacts our whole selves.

While I want freedom for attachment for you, I also want you to discover your potential that comes from your relationship with God.

We have already addressed some of the possible reasons for attachment – heart longing, low self worth, lack of love from family. Sometimes we stay attached because we are looking for the guy to complete us. Here we are giving him a much greater role than he was meant to fill. We need to recognize that we are doing that, and that in order to find completion we must look higher than him.

Before I gave my life and heart over to God, I was dominated by my desire for Luke and my need to make things right between us. Of course I was dominated by these things with other guys too, long before I even met Luke. That being said, it wasn't about Luke, it was about me. *I* was missing something inside and *I* was putting that hope on guys (without calling it that).

While I still struggled with these kinds of things later, the degree paled in comparison to what I felt and did, all the years prior to that spring day. My point is this... preoccupation with guys, various fears and the need to be in control, can be particularly high when we don't focus on Someone else, and seek Him to manage our life and feelings. More than that, our search for value and inner strength only becomes settled as we sink our hearts into God. As I've said, this time in my life was the turning point to feeling secure in myself and freed of my need for a guy.

For those of you who identify with what I'm saying, I would encourage you to consider where you have put God and what more He has for you. Those of you who have put Him first, I would encourage you to ask yourself if you are in fact living from this place and to remind yourself of what that means. I know that by focusing on God first, we will not only have a far greater hope for freedom from attachment, we will also have a far greater hope for everything beautiful in life.

Trust in His Loving Purpose

You must remember, my dear friends, that God *truly* has your best interest at heart. If He has not allowed or blessed a situation to work, it is because He cares for you and it wouldn't have been good enough. God cannot do less than pure good because His very nature is perfect. When we think we have been robbed of happiness, it is just because we do not dream as big as God does. And something better is on its way. We are not meant to settle for less, even if we are fooled into thinking that this is the best relationship we can find.

I later began to see why Luke and I were best only as friends, as did he. We looked back on times when we tried to date, and the negative or empty feelings that came from them. Of course being so close, we continued to wonder and wrestle with our feelings, but a serious relationship never did feel fully or consistently right.

Years after college, I continued to feel more secure than I did before I made God my priority. I was also no longer trying to be "with" Luke. The problem at this point, was that I still struggled with deeper feelings for him that made me feel attached. I also wondered if I *really* could ever find something better. I did have a feeling of someone else, a very specific feeling and gut-felt promise that was extremely special to me. But sometimes I would silently question if it was totally accurate...if I could have faith in something even better than what was physically in front of me. We've all been there, haven't we? It can be so hard taking our eyes off of what we know is real and isn't bad, especially when it has very good features. We always struggle with daring to hope for better. There were of course, many moments I recognized clashing characteristics with Luke and an internal sense of frustration. Yet, it is funny how our hearts are willing to look beyond those times, when closeness and enjoyable moments are also present.

Sometimes I was frustrated that I couldn't be the kind of friend I wanted to be. When Luke would mention a girl I still found myself being jealous. It was so frustrating!

When I felt deepened feelings or jealousy, I had to continue reminding myself that I did not want to be with Luke because he wasn't right for me. I had to continue remembering that someone else was right for me, just as I had felt assured was the case. I had to take the attention of my heart back, anytime it started to wander off further in Luke's direction.

Once again, the feeling I had of Luke being best as only my friend, was deeper than surface thoughts or feelings, no matter how strong they were. This also goes for the feeling I began to receive about the man I would one day be with... this was a knowing that felt right and "just there." These feelings were meant to be listened to. They were meant to guide me. They were truer than anything else.

We may not have had a physical experience of God-sent love. Not knowing its beauty, we can be tempted to settle for less. When our hearts have not yet felt the gift, we need to lean on our *knowledge* that God can and wants to bring it to us. Let us not assume that God cannot do great things and that He is not paying careful attention to the desires He gave us. He does in fact, have a special purpose for leading us away from certain people and a trustworthy plan to bring us something better.

....

I believe that the reason I was able to be so in touch with this deeper part of me that spring, was because I had a strong connection with God already. Though I grew closer to Him as a result of this event, I already had a genuine relationship with Him, where I interacted with Him and cared for Him consistently. Therefore, His Spirit was in me and I was more able to hear Him (especially if I paid attention). The greater our connection with God, the more able we are to sense things that are *truly* going on, even if they go against what we see or emotionally feel.

I speak a great deal in this book about noticing how we feel deep down. This is what I am talking about. We must learn to listen to the quieter sense in us that we often overlook or ignore. And we must be developing our relationship with God at the same time so that the sense is stronger and more easily heard.

The Lord said, "Go out...for the Lord is about to pass by. Then a great and powerful wind tore the mountains... but the Lord was not in the wind...after the earthquake came a fire, but the LORD was not in the fire. And after the fire came a gentle whisper." (1 Kings 19:11-13)

....

The Control of God

This book is about all that we can do. But it is necessary for us to know and remember that we don't have to do it all by ourselves. What I mean is, God is in control. He can make things happen in our world, all on His own.

That idea is something I never understood while I was growing up. I thought that everything that happened was a result of me and/or the other person. God was only watching us. And He could only do what I asked. Now, God needs us to ask Him to work in order to provide greater things in and for us. But He is also bigger than that. He is the one who starts a movement in us to come to Him anyway! God can do things Himself. Let's not forget that He is after all, God.

For example, my experience with Luke that spring was not random. God provided for it. In His creative mind, He gave me the opportunity to go to a higher place with Him.

Can you see Him getting involved with you? How might He be leading you through this book?

We must not think we are left alone and that everything is counting on us. The good news, is that God can come into any situation and influence it in ways we cannot. Besides the fact that God can help and influence us, He can also influence the other person. When I look back on my years with Luke, I can see obvious moments God influenced him to hold back from me, when it wasn't best for me to get more involved with him. He can create stumbling blocks that inhibit a relationship He doesn't want, and He can open doors to one that He does. If we want these things, we must specifically ask that He does them.

Now, while there are times God will specifically make something happen, there also times when He will simply use what would naturally occur to lead you in a certain direction. Consider your present situation...can you see God at all in your situation? If you think about His desire to give you a safe, good relationship that honors Him, can you see His leading in a certain direction?

It is important that we specifically ask God to take over. It can be a real relief to know that God can do what we cannot and He is affecting something that feels too big for us. God's power need not be underestimated – He can have total control over His world and it's practical, physical events.

I remember when I told God that I would follow Him and I agreed not to be with Luke. I knew I had to tell my friend that we shouldn't proceed. But the thought of approaching Luke and saying that just seemed overwhelming. I had already done something that felt huge to me and this part felt too hard. After all, so far I had only pursued him and tried to convince him to be with me. The most I felt I could do now was agree with him if he also felt that we shouldn't proceed (and I hoped he agreed with me on it). But since God had been asking a lot of me lately, I was very scared that He would also make me initiate the conversation and say it to him first. I was so overwhelmed with the thought that I had to try asking something of God. I hoped in God's grace and I asked Him to do me a favor – to influence Luke. "Lord," I said, "Please make sure that Luke feels the same way about this. And please, if there is any way, it would mean so much if you would have him say it first."

I didn't know if God would answer that request, but He did. Luke and I ran into each other two nights later and he said he didn't think we should proceed. Though he did not come to the conclusion the same way I did, God led him to it in a way that reached him personally, and through a Scripture verse. When he asked what I thought, I peacefully agreed. And boy was he surprised! We smiled and hugged each other and said what a roller coaster it had been. But we both felt a real peace. It was one that seemed strange for two people who had just given up what they wanted.

Now, I am sure many of you wish things could flow that easily between you and a guy. I have plenty of other experiences between me and guys that were not nearly as easy or smooth. But in each case, I can see God using their tendencies to move me away from them and towards a different future. And He always brings us eventually to that same feeling of peace when we listen and do the right thing.

We don't always know what to ask God to do and sometimes we can't be sure if it is what God wants, so in those cases we can just tell God we are giving it all to Him. We can be honest with the things we hope for and just say it is His decision. We just can ask that He take over and come into every bit of it. Rest in the knowledge that if you ask God to be the Lord over the details, He will be.

Thank goodness this is not all up to us!

"Be still and know that I am God." (Psalm 46:10)

....

Any person, any thing, that we surrender to inevitably dominates us and takes away our freedom. But with God it is different. The ironic thing is that *when we surrender to God, we gain our freedom.* By putting things in line with how they were meant to be, we are setting things straight. He is the only one who helps us be more of who we can be. Ironically, when we gain more of God, we gain more of ourselves.

....

Our Real Selves

You see in me someone else and I believe I can too, somewhere in the distance of the sun. She bows her head in tranquil reverie, and smiles gently, laughs a little perhaps. She is strong. And in her strength she is filled with a peace so lovely, she needs nothing else. Yes, I see her. She is so close I could reach out and....

Yes, one day....

(poem, first term of college)

As I had established, I didn't like the way a guy made me feel while growing up. The way I became angry, agitated and anxious with every move he made (or didn't make). I could see in front of me this little, weak girl who couldn't stand on her own and who let other people affect her too deeply.

But throughout this time of introspection, I also began to see a ray of hope. There was something in me deep down that told me this was not the real me. That is why I started praying for it initially. Somehow even then, I knew I would change years later. But at the time it was a strange thing to consider. The only "me" I had ever known at that point was overly emotional, sensitive and without peace. How could I think even for a moment that she wasn't really who I was? What gave me a basis for understanding that? There was a depth to that thought and I somehow felt it was real. Even as I battled the same old feelings, there remained within me a hope and subtle strength. I had a gut-level *knowledge* that there was more to me than this. Somehow if I looked deep enough, this quiet knowing felt even more significant to me than every other distracting emotion on the surface.

There was instead of a little, weak girl, a strong and peaceful woman who does not let others bring her down because she has her own internal security that no one can steal. She doesn't battle with obsessive thoughts and worries, but she is calm and at peace. She laughs and enjoys her life, not getting caught up in the details and trusting God for all of it. And one day, I somehow believed, I would find her.

"Seek first His kingdom and His righteousness, and all these things will be added unto you as well." (Matthew 6:33)

Defined by The Fall?

The result of the Fall is that we rely on ourselves with all of our shortsightedness. We are also more directly opened to unhealthy behavior, weakness and pain. The Fall prevents us from living up to our full potential, if we continue in its rebellion. Everything about it is a compromise of the free and beautiful creatures we were created to be. When I felt that I was not being who I was created to be, I was right. I was afraid of letting go, held prisoner by other's actions and my own emotions and I was limited in my abilities. I couldn't have been living up to my fullest potential.

A wonderful thing is that God never sees us as these hopeless, fallen people. He never saw me as the weak, helpless girl I thought I was. He saw me always as that woman I would later become. And He was the one who told me about her. It was His Spirit within me that revealed the truth of who I really was, at a time I wasn't feeling like her at all. He does not dwell on what we can't do or what we are doing wrong and He does not define us by those things. Instead, He focuses on the potential laid dormant within us. He sees only hope, no matter what we may see. Our potential for greatness cannot be pushed away, even if other things are put on top of it.

When Christ came for us, He opened the door for a new life. The Fall does not define us anymore because when Jesus died, He took away the human nature that was holding us back and gave us a clean slate. Now we start new. This new way of living is based on our original birth. It is full of strength, peace and wisdom. It was what I began to feel more when I invited God to take charge, but it was always there. Even when we feel overwhelmed by our weaknesses, there is still a different person within us.

Now when old temptations of worry and emotional burdens tempt me, I have a place to take them, as I again surrender. It is also much easier now, than it used to be. I remind myself of who I really am and the old self doesn't have as strong a hold on me anymore.

Just as truth belongs to God, so it is truth that He always sees. You may have seen yourself as someone you are not proud to be and someone who has little hope to be different. However, God sees the truth and essence of who you are. It is impossible for Him to define you by your sin or your struggles with it, because in His mind that is no longer who you are. He does not define you by these hard times, and doesn't want you to either. He wants you to know your true identity.

Many people wonder how they can begin to feel more of this new self in them. How they can actually *feel* stronger and better in themselves. A large part of this is choosing God first, whereby we are united to Him in a deeper way. Suddenly, something changes naturally within us, without our own tiring efforts. That is always a best first action. Secondly, we must ask His help to discover and believe in who He says we are, reminding ourselves daily of these truths so we can live from them.

When I gave myself to God I learned that the deepest change comes from Someone bigger than me. I saw that the One who created me could recreate me, in my full potential. And as I keep coming back to what has been revealed, I can continue to grow in owning and experiencing the truth of myself.

Now, while we will always have times that challenge us to continue keeping Him first, there remains nothing like the first time we begin to do it.

Do you see a greater potential within you? What does it look like and feel like?

"If anyone is in Christ he is a new creation; the old is gone, the new has come!"

(2 Corinthians 5:17)

· ·

Many people in this world think that our spiritual life is one portion of our life that stands on its own, separated from the rest of us. But that simply isn't the case. We are whole beings, a mixture of all that goes on inside. And every part of us has some sort of effect on every other part. Our spiritual growth therefore, impacts everything - our thoughts, our feelings, our every day actions. Of course it also lifts us above ourselves to connect more deeply God, who gives us a higher help to get things accomplished.

As we look into the practical steps of letting go of attachment, let us keep in mind that they have a greater power when we are really aligned with God and the truth of ourselves. Let us be sure to be addressing this core part of ourselves, so that what we do flows out of a secure inner place.

Come back to this chapter in the future, when you need to remind yourself of the importance of focusing and surrendering to God. And when you could use some reminding of the strong, joyful woman you already are.

PART 2

THE PROCESS OF LETTING GO

Chapter 6

What Letting Go Looks Like

Before you consider letting go, it would be good for us to establish what that entails. First of all, you need to realize that there is something to let go of. And that something is your emotional attachment. It is not so much the person, as it is the way you see and treat him. It is the heart-felt view that this person is more than who he really is. It is a creation of its own that encompasses your emotions and guides your perspective. It serves as the foundation from which you think and act.

Secondly, it is valuable to realize that letting go is a process. For some of you, complete freedom may appear suddenly and without much notice. But for many of you, letting go involves conscious effort and specific steps taken in that direction through time. While the struggles may continue, they do get easier. Even if you are surprised at how you may still be affected, the important thing is that your decision to respect your well being is maintained.

What it Means

Letting go means you accept what this situation is and what it is not. It means you are honest about what is missing, accept the facts and no longer dwell on them. It means taking your hands off of a situation and allowing God to take it where He wants. It means relinquishing control. To let go means taking the focus from the guy and accepting that you do not want to look for what you can't find. It is taking a step back and not stretching yourself and your heart out to the other person. It means caring for your own well being. It is taking charge over your emotions, rather than letting them take charge of you. But here is the best part, it means being free. It means having relief, joy and the opportunity to start fresh.

Letting go involves making an effort to change your behavior and thoughts so that they no longer encourage your emotional feelings around this person. There are things you can think about founded on God, peace and truth, rather than on heartfelt tendencies and fantasies. There are also actions you can take to avoid treating him in an even slightly a romantic way. These are things that help you internalize what is right and that do not tempt the activation of your attached heart.

Some of you will be able to achieve total independence from this person. The light will go on and your heart will follow your wisdom completely. Others of you, particularly those who still see this guy or who think highly of him, may not experience a perfectly unending sense of freedom without temptation. But you know that you are letting go when you are without the same heaviness of attachment. It is when you think of this person less often and whatever thoughts you have do not contain the level of intensity they used to. It also includes no longer dwelling or being preoccupied with thoughts of him. It consists of feeling freer, and more capable on your own. If rough times arise, it means being able to get through them more easily.

Finding Another Relationship?

My dear friends, I am sure you have all wondered at one point or another how much easier this road would be if you had a pleasant, comforting diversion. Maybe you are thinking about finding someone else to "help" you out. That certainly would seem nice, wouldn't it? Has anything stopped you from pursuing that idea?

I wish I could advocate a quest to find a guy right now because I want this to be as easy on you as possible. I want you to find happiness. But those are the reasons that I cannot recommend you finding another relationship at this point. In fact, I would discourage you from it. Particularly if you were involved in a recent breakup, have negative patterns or are suffering from severe attachment, there is much healing you need to do in yourself first before you can experience any healthy relationship. Even if you haven't gone through anything severe, it can always be a good thing to take time out and see what God wants to do in you as an individual.

Let me also clarify that if God decides to bring the right man into your life in the near future (wouldn't that be great?!), I am not saying you should automatically turn it down. But that you should be very prayerful and fully sur-rendered so that you can make sure it is in fact from Him. Luring temptation can come at a very vulnerable time so be careful. More likely than not, you will be rationalizing a situation if it comes at a "not so good" time and it will be best to wait.

You need to be aware of your motivations for consid-ering a new a guy (that it is not based on jealousy or to make the path easier). I would go so far as to say that you should not even consider another person until: **(1)** *Decent time has passed* after a breakup **(2)** *You feel wiser, stronger and/or renewed.* It is particularly in our key moments of distress and hardship that God can grow us and tend to us in the most powerful, life changing ways. If we ignore and side step that good work, then we bring our frailty and fears into another relationship and can likely get into another mess. And if we do not allow God the time to work in us, we often fail to grow in developing our own strengths and valuable identity for the rest of our lives. If we don't really have a healthy view of ourselves we miss out on a great deal personally and can't have a truly good relationship with anyone.

We also need God to begin loosening our ties to the wrong person because this will make more room for the right one. It will be honoring to the new person He desires to bring and it will be a fresh start for you without any pesky emotional strings.

The more you desire to find someone else in this time, the more you may be leaning on the presence of a relationship or man to define your happiness and perhaps define yourself. Dear ladies, it can be so hard to shift your focus from who you can see to who you can't. But as I have been saying, it is only God who can give you deep security and help you feel differently in yourself. Let this be a time when you choose to seek Him instead of a man, and what you want will in fact come.

Experiencing the Desire to Let Go

Of course the prospect of giving up these heart feelings for this person can be very daunting and scary. How ironic and sad that we are afraid of doing what is good for us and which results in joy.

Contrary to how it might feel, we do not give up because we recognize emotions don't matter. We do it because we know they do. We let go because they are special and real. And they deserve our care. We need to steer these powerful drives in only the appropriate, safe places for it. We loosen our grip because we know the power of the heart. We know that a situation that doesn't care for it appropriately puts us in turmoil and hurts us needlessly. We know that these situations are not worth it. And we know that we are. We know that the extravagant love God poured into our molding makes us precious and valuable. We decide to change because we know our beauty. We respect the power of our desire for love and we honor its tenderness. Simply, we guard our heart's well being because we are inherently too valuable for anything less.

> *"Above all else guard your heart, for it is the wellspring of life."* (Proverbs 4:23)

In order to strengthen the desire to let go, here are a couple steps that are helpful to take (or take again)...

1. Get a good handle on what you really want.

Think about the situation and what it does not have to offer. See it for the whole picture. Consider what is possible and what you *really* want right now. Listen to yourself... really listen. Your deepest desires will come with a sense of peace.

2. Commit to what you know is right.

Don't let your moods carry you...

I guarantee you that your feelings will change. You should expect that and know it is just a normal part of the process. You also have to be willing to commit to the right path, regardless of distractions. You must be willing to follow what you know, rather than what you feel. Remember, just because you feel something does not mean it is true.

Be aware of spiritual battles...

Whether you have thought about it or not, when we start to truly change and do the right things, we often encounter some sort of opposition. Usually in those times the enemy is trying to persuade us to go back and stay stuck. When I was trying to figure out if I should listen to God that spring, I felt a heavy feeling in the air that made me know something big was going on – not just in me but also around me. Secondly, even though I had great peace when I agreed with Luke to not proceed with a relationship, I began to feel a great deal of fear the next few months. I felt bombarded with doubts, wondering if I had done the right thing, if I should take it back, and how great it would be to have a boyfriend. These thoughts were constantly on my mind. However, as I had said earlier, we must look beneath those surface thoughts/feelings no matter how loud they are. Deep down I continued to feel a peace and strength in what I had done. And I continued to grow and experience more of my true self during that tough time which did quiet down.

We must not be surprised that these kinds of thoughts come to tempt us away from developing our potential and living new lives. And we must be willing to know they are not from God and we should not believe them or follow them.

Below are the **main points** we have discussed in the book so far. Meditate on each of these in order to be encouraged in the right direction.

- **See/listen for the whole picture and God's direction**
- **Recognize our desires cannot be fulfilled**
- **Face that the little benefits are not worth the hardship**
- **Learn to prioritize our own health and value**
- **Trust God's real presence, power, and desire to bless**
- **Consider our God-given strength/real identity**

Chapter 7

Reality and Acceptance

Seeing Things as They are

It is the nature of attachment that our vision of this person and our relationship to him is slightly misaligned with reality. We spend the time thinking of him in the tender place of our hearts. And it's easy to feel that this guy has a bigger role in our life than the one appropriate for him. It only spirals from there. We want more than the situation can offer only to get disappointed time after time. Letting go of attachment begins by seeing more clearly. It starts with distinguishing our emotionally skewed eyesight from the real dynamic of the situation and God's wisdom for it.

As I began to focus more on letting go of my attachment to Luke (I will get into this later), I recognized that I had a visual image of him that was big and with me often. It gave the impression that this guy is very important to me, a central figure in my life and more than a good friend. But as I began trying to let go, I realized that the picture in my head of Luke was not who he really was. Instead, it was who I *felt* he was to me (and what I thought I wanted). The reality is that he was not a large figure in the middle of my life. He was outside my own life, a good buddy with whom I could relate to as I would a good girlfriend.

So it is with us. Attachment can paint a picture in our minds that is contrary to what is really going on in the situation. We can feel for the guy and then see him in a way void of complete reality. Seeing this person as more than who he can be in our lives is an illusion. It is created by our emotions, the needs we look to satisfy and our blindness that creates the desire to hold on.

The Relationship as it is

"Do not conform any longer to the pattern of this world, but rather be transformed by the renewing of your mind. Then you will be able to test and approve what God's will is. His good, perfect, and pleasing will." (Romans 12:2)

Attractive Memories

Oftentimes part of your illusion is based on what you actually have seen or experienced. It may be that you remember good times with this person and those are what characterize your image of him. How many times do you sigh at considering moments of joy and/or loving connection to this person? What about when you felt closer to him than anyone and touched by a mixture of peaceful contentment and childlike excitement? Emotional desires can nurture warm moments in your thoughts so that they become the definitive memories, the foundation on which your vision of him is based. Why, sometimes it is almost as if the other moments of anxiousness, frustration and apprehensive fear don't even come into your memory! How can they when the positive memories flood your mind and you go along with the current.

Inevitably, it is in the joyful memories that we will question or forget our reasons for letting go. Our desires for remaining attached are encouraged to persist and our questions about changing become dimmer and dimmer. It is also in these times that our perception of reality is skewed. Yes, these wonderful times did happen. And let me say first, it is right that they are special to you. But by dwelling on these during attachment, we are being lured into a false reality of perfection and captured into our responding emotions that lead us to want what is not right.

While these good points and relational compatibilities are real and present, they are only a piece of the picture. Before we know it, reality is splashed in our faces like a rude, yet familiar awakening. As draining and discouraging as these moments can be, in some way they can comfort us. If part of us has felt hesitancies about being attached, then when we consider the good memories, our pleasant thoughts are mixed with subtle unsettledness about what they drive us to feel. When negative times pop back up, we can use them as reminders of what we felt we needed to do all along.

We need to open our eyes and be unafraid to remind ourselves of the hardship we have faced, the noticeable questions that the relationship has posed and the way God has spoken to us and/or guided the situation all along. We need to see the whole, real picture of a relationship before we can assess its level of rightness and be free to make the right choice about being emotionally involved.

God's Vision

Beneath whatever you feel and think you want to have, God *has* designed a specific place for this person in or out of your life. And no matter how things have unfolded, His plan is what holds true.

Please keep in mind that while God would not intend for us to have a relationship with certain people, He also does not approve of any inconsiderate way this guy may have treated you. God never wants you to be mistreated or disrespected in any form.

Now, even if this person is instead kind, Godly and wonderful, he still may not be best *for you*. You may meet a great person, but it doesn't mean he is meant to fit you in a serious relationship and as a future spouse. That is what I found with Luke.

You simply must remember that God does indeed have a wonderful plan. He has a deep understanding of your unique self and the kind of person that would complement and bless you in the way your heart deserves.

Being Friends?

A friendship is good when it brings blessing to the lives (both emotionally and spiritually) of both you and the guy and when it honors God. Real friendships are meant to deepen our enjoyment of life and encourage our inner growth.

1. The guy is a good friend for you...

My friendship with Luke was a clear blessing for years, as it developed both our potentials and lasted even when I didn't try to control it. When we were treating one another purely as friends there was great peace and a sense of rightness within us both. But in order to release some of the other feelings, I decided to not talk to him for a while until my heart felt less deeply involved. Simply, we need to listen to ourselves internally and see if we need a period of distancing before we can come back stronger and more detached.

When we are still friends with the person, maintaining motivation towards freedom can be even more challenging. Letting go is particularly not a one time deal in these cases, but needs to be kept up in the various interactions. I had to maintain my letting go with Luke since we remained friends. Even as my attachment was improving, there were times I altered how often we spoke to and saw each other to maintain my freedom. Part of letting go here is keeping tabs on yourself and having the discipline to completely hold back when needed, for as long as needed.

However, if a comfortable friend relationship ends up being too much - or too consistently - of a struggle, this man is probably not right for you in that role.

2. The guy works later as a friend...

If you have never seen this guy in friendship terms, you need to be aware of the fact that even if he may be a good friend for you, it will take time in between before that can properly occur. Don't forget that being with him or talking to him makes you feel as though you both are still together. Giving a complete rest from all interactions can be very healing and is particularly necessary at such times. And this process cannot be rushed. If you want time with him too badly, then you have not let go of your attachment. These feelings show that more time is needed.

When it comes to situations that involve attachment (also depending on the intensity) it is not very common to be close friends. A casual friendship with minimal sharing is more likely, if any at all. Oftentimes that is the healthiest option for us.

Be careful that your present or future friendship does not resemble your dating relationship. It should be far less intimate and the interactions should be sparse in comparison. If you are surprised that you never felt upset about the break up, it is a possible sign that the relationship you share with this person is too much like the romantic one. Therefore, the practical, physical aspects of letting go have not yet begun.

The question of there being a friendship and what that looks like is best left in God's hands. Ask for the help to loosen your grip, to hear His heart and follow along. Let Him take care of the situation, and see what He does. I have noticed that my friendship with Luke has not continued (or gotten better after a hard time) because of anything he or I did.

3. The guy isn't good for you to be friends with...

This scenario is a very common result in situations of attachment. It might be heartbreaking for some of you, understandably so. At the same time you hurt, there might be a part of you that is very relieved because having only a friendship with him seems too difficult. Maybe you know this is the best scenario for you. The relationship may not be possible without romance and it may cause far more pain if it were to continue in any fashion. There are also those guys who are simply toxic to be around and would only bring you down. Needless to say, it is good to be completely separate from people like that.

But maybe you just hate the idea of not having even a friendship with someone you have been so close to. Maybe you feel that way about others, like past friends, as well. I completely relate. However, there are in fact other things even more important - like your heart and your health. Oftentimes we end up giving too much power to those around us. This person is just a person. Let's remember that.

*The question of whether or not you can be friends requires that you be honest with yourself. By noticing what you feel deep down and letting God lead, you may have some idea of the answer. A real sense of abiding peace, a feeling of inner maturity and closeness to God, can often be signs that the type of relationship you share with this person is good and healthy.

A note to you on this topic....

Despite what will or will not happen, we must not get preoccupied with the future. We must live in the present moment of what needs to take place and live only there. I know women (myself included) who were able to later be friends with the guys they were attached to, but only after some time. And in that time of letting go, they had to really let him go. This meant not daydreaming about spending any time with him, even as friends.

When I was letting go of Luke, I actually told myself that I wasn't going to talk to him, period. I imagined my days and months ahead not talking to him. Whether we ended up talking or not, my visualizing not doing it made me feel freer already. Then if he called, I would take my time calling him back. If we talked I kept it at short, surface level conversations. I had to resist the urge to call if something happened I wanted to share with him and tell myself that it was fine for just me to know it. It is just my life and he doesn't have to know everything. I imagined being totally free from him in every way.

It is only when we really become free that we will have what we need later. We have to take it a step at a time. If this time in front of us calls for no involvement, then we put our minds only there. We live in the present.

When Reality Pains us

It can be so difficult when confronted with a reality you did not expect or one you desperately hoped would be different. You may feel the loss of a desired relationship that, despite your dearest hopes, was never able to come to fruition. Despite the good you could see it just wasn't enough and it hurts. These scenarios can arouse within us much heartache, disappointment and fear. It is here that our most vulnerable places surface and our real tests in faith appear.

In these painful times we can allow ourselves to feel the aching disappointment and take the time to mourn. This probably will happen the most deeply early on and then reappear in bouts at different times in the future. Be patient with yourself in this process. It is important to face what we are feeling so that it does not hinder us later, in deeper ways.

There are times in my life when I was suffering that I wished I could press a fast forward button - skip all the pain and get to the other side. But the sad truth is not only are we unable to do that, but it probably wouldn't be good for us anyway. I believe there is something done within us through the process of healing, that is vital to our future health and life equipping. This is particularly true if we approach our healing by leaning on God and requesting He indeed use the time for a higher purpose. And of course the good news is, we *do* move past the pain.

Fortunately, we have a Father who understands our anguish, our battles with blatant doubt and our tendency towards anger. It is here that we show ourselves honestly to Him, unashamed and unafraid, knowing we can be carried towards help.

We can also remind ourselves that God desires not only our highest good, but also our most complete *happiness*. Wait, God not only wants what is good for me but also wants me to be happy? Yes, He does! How often we fail to remember that. Let us remember that happiness comes from Him and no where else. We have fooled ourselves into thinking that the things He asks us to turn away from are the sources for our joy. We are the ones often willing to settle for second best, if that. We do not try for real happiness when we hold on to things that prevent our growth and joy. God is the one who wants more for us than this.

What if We Weren't Losing Much?

In some way, saying goodbye to your attachment feels similar to saying goodbye to the guy himself. The figure we have created through the energy of attachment is very real and powerful. It need not be based on reality to have inherent strength. It carries our hopes, our most tender feelings, our past and our heart. Letting go of this certain perception can involve real mourning and loss. And that is important to acknowledge, as well as experience. However, embracing the truth of the situation will also be relieving, amidst the sadness.

The distorted viewpoint of attachment may create this person, this situation, to hold more than it realistically can. Saying that we have something to lose is equivalent to assuming that we had something in the first place. What I mean by "something," is that which we have wanted. I do not consider it to be little benefits mixed with emotional unrest. Instead it is good, real and that which would hurt us to lose. It composes a material reality, similar to a physical, dense substance that richly exists. It really is *something*. Usually we do not have such a distinct composition from an incomplete, translucent image and a situation with unmet needs. This being said, we may not have had something in the first place. Therefore, we don't have much left to lose. Instead of thinking there is much benefit to be lost, perhaps we can consider that the only things to really let go of are our illusions and emotional battles.

A question lies before you. Will you take the challenge to open your eyes to the reality and God's truth and see this situation for what it is? You would be giving up the created image of this person and your relationship. That alone can be frightening. But know that you are not giving up as much as you feel. What you are giving up wasn't even really there to begin with.

Simply, it is time to focus not on what we feel we are losing, but on what we are gaining. You are now gaining a future of rest, joy and strength that makes you feel good deep inside. That is what this is all about.

Perceiving the Reality of Our Identity

"As a man thinks in his heart, so is he." (Proverbs 23:7)

This verse makes a definitive statement that sheds light on the molding power of our thoughts. They have the ability to not only shape how we feel, but how we perceive ourselves and behave as a result.

If we see ourselves as lacking value, then letting go of attachment is almost foolish or not worth it, and we will not have the resolve needed to find freedom. It may be pointless to take a stand for ourselves. The connection with this person can be prioritized above our own sense of peaceful strength. And while this is often the case even minimally during attachment, it can also reach heights that reflect a deeply deficient view of our own worth.

It is very sad to me when women feel this way. I pray that if this is the case for you, God would open your heart to the inherent, *precious* beauty that you are. Christ died for you individually, as if you were the only person on earth. And if you were the only one here, He still would have come. You are so dearly loved that the Holy Son of God gave His life *just for you.*

Sometimes, our loveliness and strength may take work to find. Not because it is not there, but because it has been covered by experiences that make us believe otherwise. Look beneath those things because they do not define who you are. Assume your right over them and don't let them get the better of you anymore.

During emotional attachment we can feel at different levels, bound to negative cycles. An image of ourselves as incapable only fuels the already existing attachment and makes us feel needy, which causes us to feel weak. If we feel we do not have strength, then we will even picture behaving in ways that show our weakness and continued attachment.

I have noticed that many of our actions are premeditated, even if only briefly…

If we want to call the guy or go over to see him, it always begins with our thoughts to do so. That being said, if the initial view of yourself is a powerless woman who is hopelessly caught in this tangle, then you will think about partaking in behavior that contributes to it. This behavior encourages your emotional struggles greatly, as it also encourages your negative self view. It makes you feel stuck and no matter your analyzing, you are still moving nowhere.

Though you may be used to doing otherwise, begin discovering yourself as God sees you. Let this be a time of new ground, of pressing into prayer, Scripture, books about your value, etc. Pay attention to the new self that you have been given, knowing it is really who you are.

Try to visualize the woman you want to be. If you were to paint an image of someone you would admire, what would she look like? What are her lovely inner characteristics and how do those show through? How does she feel each day? Dear ladies, you can be this person. In fact, chances are you are already her deep down. As you know, I envisioned certain characteristics that I wanted to have – like strength and inner security – because they were what God had originally given to me. I was drawn to them because that was what God had planned for me and what was already within. I just needed the opportunity to bring them to the surface.

Identify yourself as this person you want to be, as I did. Then before acting in certain ways, or allowing certain thoughts, see yourself as this person. From that starting point, you can imagine how she would behave. Imagine ways that leave you feeling hopeful, peaceful and stronger. If you continue to keep this image of yourself ever before you, it will be a helpful guide in your release, while also developing this person inside you.

The Man as He is

As we discussed earlier, most of us have wanted this guy to act in a certain way, and have left discouraged that we don't get what we desire.

Many times I was unfulfilled and disappointed by what Luke did or didn't do. There were moments when I expected or hoped for a certain response and failed to receive it. Sometimes I would push to have it said, however subtly, but even that failed to correct the situation. Sometimes he would still refrain from saying the longed-for words. Other times he would say them, but being that they came after much prodding I would wonder if they were genuine. If they were not genuine he might as well not have said them at all!

Now, Luke and I had many great moments as well. It makes sense why our feelings were often tempted. I was caught in this tricky place...the hard times upset me and the good times just encouraged my attachment. Yet there were times I saw him as more of a pure and simple friend. In those moments I did not need as much nor get irritated as often. Instead, I could more easily brush off our moments of clashing and differing tendencies. I loved that freer feeling.

Earlier I mentioned that I had seen Luke as being able to offer more than he could. My disappointment in certain moments showed that I thought and expected more. Or I hoped for it very much, as if it were a possible reality. The truth is that Luke did not have the capacity to act the way I wanted him to. Not because he is not a good enough guy. On the contrary, I think very highly of him. It is just that we are very different in some ways. He does not have the inclination to think as I do. He also does not want to conform to what I look for, understandably. I needed to know who he is and who he is not, and accept him for himself. I also needed to know that since we are best only as friends, neither one of us is able to give to each other what our spouses can.

As I began seeing Luke for who he is and who he is not, I appreciated him more. As I began knowing I could not expect of him and our interactions what I desire with the man I will marry, I was upset less often, with less intensity. I was freer to enjoy my friend. As I stopped trying to make him fit a mold of someone he was not meant to fit, I felt less frustration and experienced more peace. I let him be where he was meant to be. I let him be where God and my deepest heart even, wanted him. That is always the safest, smartest thing for us to do.

Because attachment can create a false perspective, the situation cannot provide what is looked for through those lenses. Your desires are unable to be fulfilled by this person and that makes sense. Any expectancy for certain things is based on seeing the relationship for something it is not. In the end, you always receive what reality is able to deliver and nothing more.

"Whatever is true…think of such things…and the God of peace will be with you." (Philippians, 4:8-9)

If you perceive the scenario through muddy waters, come to God with an open heart to identify truths. Seeing the guy through emotional lenses keeps you in bondage to lies and hinders your ability to grow. It is only when you fail to own reality and instead believe it will be changed, that you stay in a stagnant place unable to let go and afraid to give up. Avoiding truth is painful, pointless and only keeps us unhappy. Again, all things we don't want!

Journal Exercise: God always sees the truth in situations. If Jesus were physically present with you and wanting to tell you what He sees is going on, what might He say?

It is vital that you get a clear, and I mean clear, picture of what your current situation is. From seeing what it is (and is not) you must figure out if it is in fact, totally wrong for you. We start with this realistic image of what the big picture is like and then we make a decision about it being unhealthy. And we must be sure of it. If we are not sure then we can't have the drive to move forward. So at this point, get from the place where you were saying, "I think this is probably wrong," to "I know this is totally wrong and therefore not what I want."

Learning to Accept

Acceptance is key for inclining us to let go. It is only after we come to terms with the reality of a situation and stop struggling against it, that we are able to rest. Our acceptance is a powerful force which lines us up with truth and releases us of the need to create anything different. We face that fact that we cannot change what isn't changeable. And we tell ourselves that is okay.

Acceptance is about turning our attention towards the reality we may have been trying to ignore. It knows the refocusing is worth it, since what is real always surrounds us and fighting against it is tiring and pointless. We tend to believe it is our circumstances themselves that frustrate us. However, it is not simply the way things are, but *our fighting against them* that creates the hardship. It is when we let it go that we win.

We must not be afraid of the realization that this is not the place to find what we look for. If we walk away it just opens the right doors, it does not close them. You cannot bring out something that is not there to begin with. And that is alright.

Acceptance comes after we have gone through a time of hurt and grief as we face the truth and then come to grips with it. It means getting to be alright with the way things are because we realize we don't want to struggle anymore with reality. And we don't have to because there is hope for us elsewhere.

If you need to let go of anger in your heart for this person, dare to loosen your grip and release it; knowing this pain only burdens you, and does nothing productive. In actuality, we deal with people who are complex and have potentially difficult pasts and issues. Sometimes what we want is simply not there to get. We can understand that nothing was withheld from us purposefully. It just wasn't there to begin with. There is no reason to be angry because nothing that was available was denied us.

Acceptance also comes when we realize what happens does not define or reflect who we are. It appears out of an understanding that this person's actions are not about us. We are not the cause of his behavior. Therefore, it is not our responsibility to control and fix the situation or the guy, because we are not the cause of the events to begin with.

So why do we have so much trouble with acceptance? One reason is that we are afraid to face the truth. We wonder if we can still find what we look for, thereby fearing to close the door on that slim possibility. Acceptance can be very difficult because it is a form of letting go. Many people choose to continue living the illusion that they have something, and it is good enough.

Another reason for our difficulty is that we tend to have trouble trusting God. If we fail to understand His loving heart for us and His powerful ability to fulfill our desires, then why would we refrain from efforts to alter and pursue? Acceptance includes understanding that things are as they are and that is okay because God is in charge. He knows best. What is occurring is not arbitrary. We can learn from it and let it take us somewhere better.

We can also have trouble accepting due to our pride. We think that putting our distress or anger to rest means we make the decision that our treatment was fair or justified. Under this mindset we continue to carry the heavy burden of negative emotions upon us. The fact of the matter is that acceptance is not about making a right or wrong judgment call. It is simply acknowledging what exists in a given situation and not needing to burden ourselves with painful feelings about it. It is in fact for our personal benefit.

Can we come to a place of acceptance even amidst the turbulent emotions we've experienced so far? Yes, we can. We can get closer to acceptance after we have felt the emotional grief that this situation will not offer us what we desire. When these feelings are addressed and not ignored. And then we make the decision to move past them.

In summary, acceptance is achieved when we recognize that a situation or a person does not have the capacity to be what we look for. We notice that our needs cannot be met in this guy and it is not worth the struggle. And that it is a natural fact which makes absolutely no statement about our own worth. From here we make the decision to get the upset out of our system, and move on. We ask for God's soothing, His inner rest and trust that He is who He says He is and will in fact provide for the future. Now we have the ability for release and the hope to move forward.

Chapter 8

Making the Decision

Choosing to Get out of the Middle

Painted by Emotions

The interesting thing is that we assume – or want to assume - it is possible to safely remain in the middle place of attachment: being between a secure, healthy relationship and none at all (connected through attached feelings). We assume that this is a solid, actual position to be in and a life can truly be built around it. Attachment can make us feel we at least have something we can depend on. And it confuses us into thinking we can stay that way. But at some point or another, something happens…things get too tough or the other person does something new; and we get hurt. In attachment our awakened desires cannot be met consistently and safely. Any feeling of security in attachment is a false disguise and it comes and goes.

But we try to rationalize due to our fears of changing things. We allow our emotions to do what they tend to do… easily overtake our thoughts and heart, guide our behavior and be the authority for satisfaction. These emotions naturally tend to assume position over our reasoning abilities.

Oftentimes, we think only about the present moment and reason that this action is fine because it only occurs right now. We fail to consider the future ramifications. We try to be naïve (even if only subconsciously) and we succeed. How many mistakes have been made due to ignoring what could happen afterwards? Instead, we need to face what we are doing and what will happen as a result. We need to incorporate our God-given wisdom in order to get where we need to be.

God's Secure Design

A middle place is not intended by God. He knows it leaves us in a see saw of motion between anxiety and joy, unfulfilled temptation and inevitable suffering. We are simply meant for more than that. Only dependable, secure, continuous love and safety is what He wants and if you could paint the perfect picture, it would also be what you would pick for yourself. God has designed this person to have a very specific role in your life. And it isn't meant to be a messy, complicated one.

I will never forget a time with Luke years after our first discussions of dating, when we both struggled again with wanting to be together. Though this felt common to both of us, it seemed to be no less difficult. While we had our weaker moments, there came a night when he stepped up and took the courage to say what needed to be said. He told me that this middle place was not good for either of us. He said that even though we were afraid to close the door, we needed to just shut it for our own emotional well being. He also pointed out that we needed to have greater faith in God. I was relieved that he said what I was thinking, but was too afraid to vocalize. I respected Luke very much when I heard those words because I saw within them his strength, wisdom and Godly character. Of course, the moment was sad and difficult as well. That feeling is unavoidable and understandable at such a time. But it also felt more peaceful and more right than anything else.

By nature, the middle is not a strong enough place to hold you. You will have to make a choice sometime. It is not a substantial, solid place created by God and it simply cannot last. While it may feel safer to not trust God enough to let go, while it may seem that going out on a limb for Him is the more wobbly place, it is the exact opposite. In fact, it is only the place of surrender and freedom that provides real security and protection.

This position is not only hard on you it can also be hard on this person. If he struggles with his feelings, you are not helping him by continuing to act in ways that keep you both in limbo and play with your emotions. I realized that more fully with Luke – that if I really cared about him I would not make things complicated for his heart. Think about yourself in choosing safety, but also think about the person you care about. May God help you with courageous trust and Christlike love.

Choosing to get out of the middle is no less than a determined, distinct choice. It is about taking authority over your thoughts and actions. If you have been trying to do this and feel stuck, you must make petitioning God a priority. You must make it your focus now to pray and spend quality time with Him until you start to *feel* more able. God gave me a feeling of ability and strength I never had before, when I was able to make the decision to let go in a serious way. He will do the same for you because it is His desire for your life as well.

Choosing Freedom

The reason we spent an earlier chapter on what you want, is because this alone will be the driving force for your decision on how to live. We do not recognize the power of a decision when backed up by desire. I used to believe that I could not decide about my feelings and that they operated outside of my control. In some cases, this is true. But while feelings can be very hard to manage, we do have much more of a say in maintaining them than we realize.

Now for making that choice...our starting point must be on the solid rock of our relationship with God and His great help in us. From here we make a decision to change, as we connect our realizations with our desire and our will. And suddenly, we have a powerhouse that few can contend with.

Let me say that if we have not made a decision, that in and of itself is one. If we have held off on making a judgment call in order to see what happens, we have already decided to stick it out. In this case, we allow our noticeable wants to outweigh our deepest wants and our needs. Staying in emotional attachment is always a choice. As long as we prioritize the little benefits we receive from it, we will stay locked in an old, stagnant pattern, and growth will not be an option. But if we choose to move towards something better then more is *always* possible.

When Does it Happen?

Much of our motivation for choosing detachment occurs when we realize we are hurting. Perhaps we are now faced with an event that creates more hardship and it wakes us up. Suddenly, the pain overshadows the limited benefits that once kept us going. When this occurs, a choice to continue in attachment or change is before us. A door opens and we can choose if we are going to walk through it. Then there are times when nothing different has happened, but internally something has changed. We just see more clearly. We begin seeing the situation in a more realistic light and realize the negatives are not worth it. Again a door opens, and we can choose to walk a different path. We are often given various opportunities when we feel that letting go is perhaps manageable. We have to be ready to finally take one.

Despite my holding on, there were times when I would allow my knowledge of what I needed to do, to influence my behavior. I would hold off from calling Luke when I wanted to. Or divert my attention when focusing on him. This was a matter of my will and it was hard. But the little bit of freedom I experienced after making myself hold back showed me the beauty of peace. And that good feeling motivated me in later moments. In fact, the more I would try to let go, while initially harder, the more contentment and strength I would end up feeling. The times I allowed myself to slip back in a moment of weakness, however, reminded me of the discomfort and childishness I used to have. I could see the difference between how it felt being attached and being free. And being free felt infinitely better!

Then there came a time when Luke began talking quite a bit about a girl he was becoming close to. I was consumed with thoughts about her, my own feelings of sadness and jealousy. I wished I could stop thinking about their relationship but I couldn't. I then knew I had to let go of my extra feelings for him in order to find relief. I thought about the pain and personal frustration I had gone through the past many years and I knew I really did want it to finally be over. I knew I was worth more than those unhealthy experiences. I considered moments I had given too much, times I did not get what I wanted and ways I still kept trying. I thought about the past years of fear, neediness and frustrating distress. I considered the weakness and unhappiness I had felt within myself. I thought about how long it had all lasted. And something hit me....I was fed up with it.

Now, I have felt unhappy with my attachment before, but in a very different manner. In the past I felt frustrated with what I could not do and I saw myself as weak. As I saw myself in those terms, I could not act in any other way. However, this time I recognized my strength. I saw that I was capable of detachment because I am not incomplete, but secure. I didn't like that I was acting weakly, but I knew I could act differently. I knew I was someone different. I knew that God's mighty, peace-filled Spirit resided within me. I felt fed up with past habits. I was fueled with the knowledge that I was more than this and that better living was possible. I knew that now was a chance to grow further into the potential that was in me.

Through feeling fed up and knowing my capacity for more, I *wanted* to let go. I *totally* wanted it. I awoke to the fact that this wasn't worth it. It was more burdensome than comforting. For the first time, I prayed with that kind of conviction. I came to God and I was sure of what I needed to do. I did not just ask for God to help me, I told Him what I wanted; knowing He also wanted it for me. I said, "God, I want to let go of Luke and I am doing it." I went on to ask for help for specifics and for His power over and in me. Never was I so sure that this is what I was going to do.

When we come to Him being sure of what we want (and mind you, I know God gave me the ability to be sure in the first place) and it is what He wants as well, we are exercising a power to move things in that direction. Our determined desire and will, when united with God's desire for us, is a mighty place to begin.

As the days went by, my resolve remained. I focused on this topic in prayer and God honored my request for help. Now, I can't say it was all smooth sailing. The old feelings returned at times and I might even sit with them for a little while. I would pray in these times, even if just for a second. I would pray for the strength and desire to get up and try again and persevere. But through time I had bigger ups, less downs and far less of a desire to pursue in thought or action. I continued to remind myself of God's faithfulness, my well being and my desire to live "better" than I had been. I was fueled by His Spirit and a conviction for emotional health. Every time I felt temptation towards my old habits, I would say to myself, "No more of this. I have done it for too long." Sometimes I would just say, "Nope!" It was amazing to watch the power of my will (as fueled by God's own) restrain not only my behavior, but also my heart.

A solid decision is powerful, as is real determination. When we *really* know what we want and refuse to waver, we have real strength. While using that vision as a guide, deep things will start to happen. Even the inside of us begins to change. We are freer, stronger and wiser.

You see, if we are unsure of something, we can easily be tossed back and forth. We can't let go and really accomplish it, if we aren't sure that's what we want to do, what we have to do, etc.

God recognizes the power of a decided heart, but He loves us too much to control us and disregard our freedom. He does not "make us" different unless we pursue asking Him to. Letting us decide is a loving, growth promoting gesture of God. Parents teach their children right from wrong and show respect by letting them make their own choices in later years. It can only be hoped that they will be wise in their decisions, strong in their resolve and unafraid to seek help.

If we ask for God's help but have not completely decided what we want to do, then we are making half of a decision and that is not good enough to change the strong currents of our emotional tendencies. Now, of course we should and need to pray for the *desire* to let go. The great thing about this kind of prayer is if we make it, we are already beginning to realize we want to be free.

Enjoying the Journey

It is important to realize that letting go is not just painful or stressful. It can also be something you truly *enjoy*. Yea, you heard me...enjoy. Don't you realize that is the reason you let go? You will feel better than you did before? I know because I have felt distinct moments of great relief. You enjoy gaining what is right and emotionally beneficial - seeing yourself grow in internal security and personal satisfaction.

Once you begin getting out of that cycle of holding on, the release will truly feel *nice*. Of course there will be hills you have to climb over as memories or circumstances arise. I wish that were not the case, but I must be honest about it. However, every time you get over them, more joy is around the bend! Always remember that.

When your old habits tempt you, God is there to offer deep strength and make it feel possible. Then you will begin to see the emotional benefits of letting go. You will experience a sense of content accomplishment and you will admire the person you are feeling within. The peace and strength you will begin to feel will make your attachment look more unnecessary and less of a temptation than it ever was before. You will start thinking, *why didn't I do this earlier*?

How You Go about it

When I was praying for the help to let go, I admitted that I did not know exactly how to go about it. What were the steps? How was I going to fight my old habits? Also, I wasn't sure how my desire to let go would stay on track, even when I no longer felt "fed up."

Listed below is a summary of the main points discussed so far that God gave me for letting go. They helped me be refreshed in the right decision when faced with temptation. I suggest that you think deeply and honestly about each directive. While you can do them in this order, they do not need to be in this sequence. Listen internally to which step you need to do next. Chances are you will jump around at different times depending on your mood and daily circumstances.

Meditate on these ideas as you feel you need to. Always come back to them. It can also be helpful to write down your thoughts while you process them.

- **Recognize how your attachment hurts you**

- **See things as they are and as they are not**

- **Accept the reality of the situation**

- **Shift focus from the guy to caring for yourself**
    - o   *I will discuss this in the next chapter

- **Trust God...His love and His power**

Chapter 9

Shifting Focus

As described earlier, we think too much and too often about this man. We are overly concerned with what is going on in his life and how he relates, or may relate, to us. We consider what he is doing or what he isn't and our mental energy is wasted over the same arguments and analyzing.

Since attachment involves a consuming attention on the other person, if we alter our focus and redirect it to ourselves, we already accomplish a great deal in the way of freedom. Shifting our attention can be a releasing state in and of itself and it can lead more easily into behavior that encourages it further. If we truly tend to ourselves, then we are naturally drawn to healing our wounds and prioritizing our needs for health. We can then move more easily towards thoughts that free us of unhealthy feelings and promote our well being.

Let me begin encouraging your new focus by saying that *letting go has nothing to do with this person.* You heard me...it has nothing to do with him. It has only to do with you.

Attachment grabs our attention and places it on the guy, but despite our preoccupation with him, the results and process of attachment is about us and takes place within us. We need to take back our unhealthy "other" focusing.

Yet we must focus on ourselves in the right ways. As we have already discussed, our attached view can incline us to believe that whatever we receive from the other person is a reflection of who we are and what we cause. But the other person and the situation is far too complex to be a direct result of our nature. Making our opinion of ourselves dependent on the treatment we receive is simply based on lies and creates unnecessary baggage. Instead we must learn to have our own, unshakeable opinion of who we are simply in ourselves and unaffected by this person. We consider our growth potential, our strengths and values, and God's vision for us, which are all based on His truths. We end by concluding we deserve kind treatment as well as self-care and peaceful living.

Separating Ourselves

Now we do think about ourselves in attachment, but often in collaboration with thoughts about him. Our personal opinions are affected by his actions, his seeming mindset. We do not focus on ourselves independently from this person and from the relationship, enough of the time. If we do, there is only a part of ourselves that is seen as a completely separate entity. We may not see the guy as part of who we are, but as an interrelating force in our inner self and life.

Let me illustrate. Picture a large circle with your name in it. This is you and your life. Around you are multiple circles, each representing a family member and close friend. Further out from them are people with whom you are less close to. This guy, however, shares a piece of the center circle *you* occupy. You feel this on various levels even if you may not consider it in such a way. For example, when something goes on in your life, you think of him and want to share it. You desire the same thing in his experiences. He occupies your thoughts even when you think of your own particular life situations that you currently go through. Likewise, you wonder very often about his life events. In some way you are sharing yourself with this person in ways that you share yourself with no one else. Look to see how differently you consider this guy with regard to other people in your life. Recognize that it is most appropriate for your circle to contain just you and other people to be external figures with whom you simply interact.

Being attached to someone inclines us to mold our living at some level around theirs. We have forgotten to make our own life the center of attention and instead it becomes a sort of side event around the guy, or around your interactions with him. What it comes down to, is that we fail to focus on our self in our own right, most of the time. The clarity of our independence is compromised and we forget how much of our own person we are *in every way*.

Before you make any move towards health then, you must shift the focus of your attention to yourself. Think about this a moment. Have you ever asked yourself, and I mean really asked yourself, "How am *I* doing?" Never mind about what the guy will think or do… *what about you*? What is going on in you and how are *you* feeling?

I rarely asked myself that question. Not to say that I wasn't aware of my own pain and dissatisfaction; nor my times of freedom and my insight to truth. I have always been self aware and able to notice what I experience internally. But it was rare that I so distinctly shifted focus as to not concern myself at all with what I would stir in or get from Luke, and instead considered solely myself. It was rare that I focused simply on me and how I was doing, while not simultaneously focusing on the situation. It was not often that I made *my* feelings and *my* well being a priority. That I looked deep down, asked if this was good for me, and allowed the state of my health to matter more than anything else around me.

Putting your deepest need for health first is taking care of the person God loves and intentionally created. It is honoring His perspective of your value. You have a right to make yourself a priority because your well being *is* the most important. God made you a beautiful, deep soul who was worth giving His life over to rescue. How completely cherished you are! Treat yourself with at least that much caring respect.

Let me say again, friends, this is not about him. This roller coaster of a dilemma is not about who he is or is not, and your path towards healing is not about him either. You are the one who is hurting and who battles unrest, the one whose strength and joy is compromised. It is your heart on the line, your weaknesses being wrestled with. It is time to focus on simply you and tend to yourself from there.

Even if you know he is having a hard time, it is your job to take care of yourself. God said to "**Love your neighbors as you love yourself**" (Matthew 22:37-39). The prerequisite here is that you love yourself. That is your starting place.

You also have authority over yourself and no one else. You cannot control another person. Your actions and responses are the only things you can be responsible for.

Notice what is going on inside. After being aware of this, ask what you can do to help yourself feel better. If what you find is a small, scared little girl, then deal with what is there. Tend to her and guide her towards the freedom that will be her strength. Care for your own health by seeing how you might take care of yourself from this point.

One thing I caution you to guard against, is trying to display your freedom to this guy in an effort to have him see you as strong and admirable, or in an effort to stir feelings of jealousy. While a feeling towards this can be natural, it needs to not be pursued. Otherwise, your focus remains on him and your welfare stays undermined and damaged. "Letting go" *for* him means you are not really letting go *of* him. Plus, the benefits you could receive from real freedom will be unattainable. Do this and everything about this, for you.

Finally, let us be clear that focusing on yourself, particularly when you are not used to it, can be very healthy and important. It grows your sense of well being and creates more inner health. It also will impact your future relationships (romantic or not) for the better. I'll give you two reasons for this...

One, you need a sense of individual identity. Even when you are with the right person, you need to know who you are and not look to him to complete you. Even good relationships can be damaged if one or both people are overly dependent on each other and don't know who they are apart. Two, if you don't really appreciate yourself you cannot love other people the right way. It is only from knowing your true value that you can have the fuel to care for those around you in a way that encourages their potential while maintaining your own. It is there that you have the capacity to see the good in those around you, while accepting their limitations and tending to their hearts appropriately.

Remember, *this is your life*. It is yours alone. You *can* do something about how you feel and what happens, good or bad. You are meant to take care of yourself.

You are your own person and you do not occupy the circle with this guy. If you have the desire to share what has just happened in your life, take a breather. Tell yourself that he doesn't need to know. It doesn't matter if he does or not. You don't need his response and you don't need his opinion. In fact, you don't need anything from him.

Tending to Ourselves

How often we fail to give ourselves the kind of childlike fun we need! Pursuing avenues that we enjoy, whether they be hobbies or time spent with our favorite people, can be uplifting for our souls. They can not only rejuvenate our energy, but also take our minds off of our needless dwelling.

Consider the things you enjoy doing the most. What kinds of activities bring you a smile and sense of peaceful contentment? How can you get involved in these avenues? What about places you like to go or have hoped to visit... this can be as simple as your favorite park or restaurant, or as immense as another country. What is both possible and comforting for you? Having a weekly outing and/or times throughout the week to pursue these activities and places you enjoy can be a great diversion.

You can also think about what motivates you and encourages your sense of ability. Maybe you want to start training to compete at some event. The process of strengthening yourself can build not only your physical body, but your emotional and mental states as well. It can be a wonderfully empowering experience.

All the same, there are even simpler ways to get in touch with that strong part in you. Is there a song that you love to sing or dance to (and nobody has to see you do it!) that fits your situation perfectly or that passionately describes breaking free and taking that courageous route? Then sing and dance your heart out! Do it whenever you want to. Remember the words and think about them when around other people, if it helps.

Reach out to friends you can trust in the times you could use that support. If you find yourself shutting out people that love you, it only makes things needlessly more difficult. It also puts you in a rut that's hard to get out of. Everyone needs the help of caring friends. Allow them to just be there for you and let them know that their presence is something you could use. Share your tough times with them. But also choose to have fun in the time you spend together. Watch a few movies you love, go out for your favorite dessert; talk and laugh about old, funny memories.

It could also be good to get involved in volunteer activities. I personally, love to be around animals. They are very therapeutic for me, so I sometimes volunteer at places that house rescued pets who need adopting. Whatever your area of interest, volunteering can be a great way to get your mind off your own stuff and bring you a sense of meaning.

You have probably thought of this before, but let me remind you not to let this hardship rob you of the enjoyment you can still have in life. If finding happiness even in the things you once loved has been hard, bare with yourself and be understanding. But also keep on doing those things, even if they are not what they used to be. It will in fact, make the road easier. And you will find that joy again. You can make the journey as painless and possible when stopping at places that offer some refreshment.

Your Value and Purpose

We need to realize that we cannot complete ourselves in any relationship. Nor do we need any relationship to make our lives even a little more important.

If you find yourself clinging desperately to someone for fear that you will not be enough without him, you are sorely mistaken. Your concern is understandable and my heart goes out to you. But as I said earlier, as long as you try to find yourself in the company of someone else you will come back empty. Dependence on another person for your own worth is a pointless venture that can never succeed. No one but God can give you that much.

The good news is that you *are* indescribably important, simply on your own. You are unique and there is no other person in this world exactly like you.

Did you know that there is also a special purpose for you to fulfill in this life? You are able to impact this world for the better. You simply may not have tapped into that potential yet. God has a plan for you to bring, to create and develop certain events in this world that will reflect His good nature and can be accomplished only by you.

Maybe you are a born artist that brings beauty, maybe a kindhearted person to show His care, maybe an implementer who makes ideas take shape, maybe a future leader in ministry. If you look inside and think about it, what potential do you see for your life? Remember God uses your weaknesses, so don't think for one moment that they limit you. In fact, oftentimes it is our weaknesses that end up becoming our greatest strengths. Take me for example...God uses my experiences not only to grow me but also to help me touch others with the truths and hope He has brought into my life.

Simply, there is an inherent value in your being and God just rejoices over your special traits. You truly do not need anyone to increase your value in any way.

No matter how you have seen yourself or what experiences with others you may have had, these are only trustworthy if they are grounded in the truth of His perspective. The more you take a chance to trust in yourself as you are, the more you will be able to feel grounded in the beauty of your real self.

Releasing Worry about Him

Not only may you focus on how this person's life may affect yours, you also may be too concerned with his own well being. Since I have the personality of a typical therapist, I've always noticed care taking tendencies in me. Perhaps some of you have the same kind of desire to look out for others and are prone to worry about them. The fact that I felt emotionally about Luke only intensified this natural tendency. I worried about his possible trials and felt it was my responsibility to divert them. While my concerns were understandable given my nature and not exclusive to the problem of emotional attachment, they were heavier and more consistent because of my attached feelings.

Trying to guide another person's life is out of our league and always unsuccessful. We cannot live someone's life for them and wanting to help too much can make us almost think we have the ability to.

Part of being a good friend is not only being there in times of need, but also trusting that this person is capable. As you have seen, Luke is a strong, Godly man. I have respected him often for it. Rather than allowing concerns over human weakness to be the focal point, I needed to remind myself of my friend's many abilities and of God's presence with him. I needed to believe in those things.

We also help the other person and ourselves when we surrender to God as the ultimate helper. I rely on prayer when I am concerned for those I care about. I ask for faith and tell God I am giving my concerns to Him because I can't carry them. I am powerless to create real change, anyway. I remind myself that God is completely able to create the change that is needed, all on His own. I pray that He take care of things in detail and I have seen God act in faithfulness to these prayers. He always brings me back to the relieving fact that He can do anything, and that He fully desires to intervene for the person I pray for. Therefore, when I go to Him the results of peace and unburdening do in fact follow.

I also had another kind of worry. I actually worried about how Luke would feel if he saw me getting over him. There were moments of experienced strength, or excitement about my future husband, when I actually felt guilty to admit to Luke that I was doing well. I would wonder if I was hurting his feelings. I have always been very concerned for his sense of contentment that if I had to, I would put it above my own. I have been overly concerned with his well being (and not as much with mine). That is ironic, considering the fact that sharing my success would only help Luke let go as well, and *that* is truly looking out for his well being. But often we do things for people that satisfy their surface desires and are afraid to address the deeper, long term ones for whatever momentary discomfort it may cause.

Those of us who are natural caretakers will have the hardest time in this area. We are usually concerned about others' feelings and put the responsibility on ourselves to be in charge of them. We put our desires in second place to their possible reactions, though they may not try to do the same for us. And we can be afraid to temporarily hurt their feelings, even if what we are doing benefits them in the long run.

Again, we need to start by grasping the idea that it is not about him. Nothing that God is growing us into, nothing about our personal struggles and calls to improvement, centers upon the guy. We have to work from the focal point of "me." And put no hindrance on our movement towards realized potential. Second to that, we need to watch out for the best interest of someone we care about.

I am of course not advocating needless discussions with the guy in your life that you know will be painful for him. My concern for Luke's feelings was based mostly on my own unfounded fears (since he is inclined to be more practical than emotional) and on my knowledge it might be semi challenging for him. But if you know a certain kind of sharing would be hurtful and is unproductive, then for his sake you need to refrain from sharing; at least for now. Also, make sure you do not speak about an idea or event in order to produce his jealousy and attention.

Finding More in Ourselves and God

I hate to break this to you all, but it is a fact that even the man who is right for you will not satisfy your every desire and longing perfectly. Now, let me assure you that God has handpicked this man for you and he will fit you wonderfully - better than any other person you have yet found. He will touch your heart with the balm of love and grant you the sweet intimacy you have missed. He will complement you better than anyone you have ever known. However, this man is human just as you are. He has certain flaws, and you will have to accept him as imperfect. On top of the beautifully sublime moments, you will have times of blatant frustration, sore disappointment and raw anger. You will have with your joyful moments, arguments and silent withdrawal. Even the best marriage will be real work and hard at times. What will you do when your desires for total, loving care and constant understanding have gone unfulfilled?

You must be first aware that this is a natural occurrence and then you must have a secure love and respect for yourself. You need to be prepared to accept this man's flaws and what he does not have the capacity to give, knowing you also are unable to give him everything he needs. Neither one of you is perfect or meant to supply for the other person all that God is meant to. You need to look to yourself for a sense of peace when he doesn't offer it and a sense of worth in times he does not display admiration. Also, you need to stand up for the respect you deserve, if you are not receiving a genuine flow of care or kind treatment.

You do these things by seeing yourself through Christ's eyes and by paying close attention to (even if you can't always feel) His mighty Presence inside of you. Your strength, your rich value and your delicate beauty come from Him. They are a constant river within you that is never affected by your moods or the man's actions. The more you pay attention to it, the more you will experience its reality.

Simply, your focus should never be completely on another person. Whether you are looking to your spouse to fulfill your every need, or doing everything in your power to serve him and his well being, you can find yourself in an unhealthy, growth preventing position. *We* are the projects God has given us to tend to and build. While relationships are truly gifts that we are meant to care for, we need to remember not to give all of ourselves to the other person. If we do, we lose a sense of our unique identity, our calling towards peace and our individual potential in Christ. We also forget to look for our meaning and life in God.

The great thing about battling our tendencies to put others above ourselves is that little by little we are stripping away an unhealthy comfort spot that needs to be removed. Every challenge we face and work through, even ever so slightly, is a valuable opportunity to be blessed in growth and future satisfaction.

Gazing at God's Perfection

By now we have seen that focusing on God is a necessary and deeply valuable road towards real peace and self-worth. Even the act of considering God can be touching and lovely. He is the source from which all other loves flow. He is like a rose and all other evidence of love in this world, like its petals. Without Him, we would have nothing beautiful.

God always knows what to say to us. He will never lose patience with us like other people; He is always gentle. But when we need to see something He knows just how to make it clear. He is at heart a comforter and a life giver. He is strong and has the power to overcome anything around us. He is our Savior. When we need to find shelter, we can call on His name and know we are under His wings. He is our refuge. We can rejoice in such a perfect presence that is always there for us. He can nourish us in a way like no other, reaching down to the depths of us that only He can see. He touches the core of our hearts. When we need someone to help us, to *really* help us, He is able. He is always thinking of each one of us with total focus and dedication. We can thank Him for His tenderness. We can appreciate His understanding, His unconditional love and His constant knowing that we are more.

It is with God that we have enough. Instead of placing your identity on the thoughts of you in a relationship with this guy, place it on you in a relationship with God. During attachment, you are stripped away from your own sense of strength and feeling of inner beauty. However, by gazing towards God and how He relates to you, you really find what was missing. When you focus on God, you gain your life comfort and your sense of self.

We may not have much experience looking to God for so much. It can seem easier to look to things we can see. But I assure you, even if what you see gives you instant and strong feelings, these emotions lack a depth and a beauty and consistence. Even if you need to practice looking to God, the reality of His nature will become much more tangible, much more of an experience, as you seek it out. Then it will in fact reach you in a deeper, more fulfilling way.

Journal Exercise: *Imagine Jesus is lovingly talking about you to our Father. What would He say? .... What does He want to say to you, that your heart needs to hear from Him?*

Chapter 10

Techniques

The attempt to let go may seem intimidating, not only because of battling desires, but also because the road to release may be unclear and the steps along the way, unknown. Here are some specific tools that have helped me and can create a successful walk towards your own well being.

1. Choosing Thoughts

Much of my purpose for helping you understand the dynamics of attachment and inner desires is to affect your thinking. Our thought processes are integral in molding our behavior and our hearts. Whether they seem automatic or deliberate, the things we think about hold great power over our lives. Attachment is strongly influenced by our thoughts. I recall asking myself if I would feel so attached if I did not think about Luke as much. And I ventured to say that I wouldn't. Luke is quite different from me in that if a situation bothers him, he refuses to dwell on it. He finds letting it go manageable. It has been helpful to learn from this ability of his.

If we are opening ourselves to truths and meditating on them, we then have the opportunity to relearn bad habits and integrate what is real into our thinking. This new way of thinking then affects our feelings, actions and life events.

Thoughts that Keep Coming

Have any of your friends ever said to you, "Just stop thinking about him!" Or when you are dwelling on a particular matter, "Why don't you just let it go?" Chances are you have also said it to yourself. It seems so simple, doesn't it? *"Just let it go."* The words and the logic behind them seem to make so much sense that any person would have to follow through. Then why can't you stop thinking, even about the things that hurt you? Maybe you decided long ago you don't want to dwell on him as you tend to. Maybe you know he has never thought about you to that extent and you have always thought about that! Or have you ever thought to yourself…"Okay, I'll let him go." But you have thought it so many times that you are obviously *not* letting him go? Sometimes even in the decision to open our fearful grasp and step back we spend so much time thinking about it, that our freedom remains immaterial.

The feeling that you can't move from these thoughts is normal. The confusing frustration over not being able to do what makes sense is normal. It is not healthy for us, but it is natural. Since thinking about the guy comes from attached feelings, having mental peace can be hard.

Yes, thinking about the other person feels seemingly automatic, especially when we are used to it. However, what we do with the thoughts that come, while challenging, is up to us. Mental freedom and letting go comes only from being intentional and determined. It comes after you have realized that dwelling is not a benefit to you after all; and that you don't want it. It happens when we recognize these are *our* thoughts and we can do something with them. We can choose to exercise power over them.

Do I Learn from Dwelling?

One question I had as I began seriously letting go of my friend was whether or not I was supposed to analyze my thoughts of him more and figure it all out. Just as it sounds now, this idea seemed vague to me, but I wondered if processing through it was necessary before being free was possible. Yet, I didn't know how to go about this or what to dissect. I prayed about what to do while feeling the weight of emotion and overanalyzing hold me down. I was also upset about things I had done recently that I didn't feel were best. I thought about what I should have done differently. But so far I wasn't feeling any better.

Then God touched my heart and showed me something else. I was thinking that if I figured out or fought against what I didn't want to do, that I would win the battle and alter myself. But I was wrong. Instead of getting closer to creating what was positive, I was actually creating more of what is unhealthy by spending time focusing on it. Even when we spend the energy pushing against something negative (like beating myself up over what I had done wrong) we can become consumed by it. Never mind that we think something is wrong (though that is very important). It is still being offered much time and mental anguish, so it feels significant. Letting go of what is unhealthy becomes even harder when we cling to it. Rather than dwelling on what has happened, we should think about *what we can do from here* that is positive and healthy. Put your energy on visualizing the good that will come from now on. Imagine doing what is right and you already start to create it.

Secondly, I had nothing to figure out. I had known deep down for years that Luke belonged purely as my friend. I knew that I felt attached most of the time, that I felt weighed down and needed the release of internalized truth. I knew I needed faith and a sense of confidence. I knew that this attachment was not good for me. I knew that I wanted him to be more than he could be. I knew that deep down I wanted my own freedom, as well as the person God designed for me. I had nothing else to figure out. But when we have so many thoughts and emotions flooding a particular situation, we are not sure if they each need to be considered, or if there is more to work through.

Now, let me point out that if you have never spent time critiquing the unhealthy things that you do or allow, then you need to be aware of them and look into them carefully. You may need to ask yourself what you haven't pondered before, what is going on, etc. It is only when you have done this often and now find yourself in a pointless, unproductive cycle, that you need to move on.

Part of my problem in not thinking was based on my usual dilemma of how to refrain from thoughts of Luke in the first place. Dwelling became automatic for me long ago, and I did not *choose* to think about him, I just did. But here is the clincher…no matter how easily these thoughts assume residency, we are the ones who allow them to stay. Of course evicting them requires a conscious choice and deliberate effort. But this is in our power, even if we are not used to exercising that authority. We can get better at it with practice.

Ways to Redirect our Thoughts…

1. Remind yourself of the truth

Just as chapter seven describes, our feelings can paint an altered view of the situation that only encourages more emotional involvement. It is important for us to always remind ourselves of the reality that is before us. Write down the true nature of this relationship and read it in times of struggle. It is also very helpful to go back and read old journals where you had written down your hesitations and/or your problems with the guy as they were taking place.

2. Put away objects that remind you of him

Whether they are photos, letters or something that belongs to him, each one of these easily has the power to capture your thoughts in his direction. Particularly items that carry great weight and remind you of emotional times need to be put out of sight. How can you try not to dwell on him when the gift he gave you stands out in your room? Or you turn to walk towards your dresser and photos of his face flash before your eyes? Be honest with yourself about what needs to be put away for your own sense of peace, well being and ability to start fresh.

3. Surrender your worries

There can be many details to make us anxious, many ideas that create concern and fear. Reminding ourselves of God's trustworthy role and our calling to rest, can help us give away our burdens. We can choose to surrender. We can let go of the thinking that we must fix, control or continue holding on. We can let ourselves relax. When we remember that God is in charge and He is caring for us, we can let it all go to Him. Peace comes from *releasing* our efforts from: the realm of outcomes, the man's thoughts and actions, the need to pursue. We can have greater rest when we look to God and tell Him to take our concerns, believing He can take care of us.

4. Correct a memory in your mind

If you find yourself dwelling on a memory between you and this person, particularly if it is a romantic one, change what happens in the memory as you re-visualize the event. Alter the situation so that instead of it turning into the emotional moment that actually occurred, you now imagine it to have happened in a better, healthier way.

For example, let's say you remember a dinner the two of you shared when you talked about getting back together. You realize now that this decision was wrong. Yet, you remember that night as being one full of hope and joyful possibility. Just thinking of it brings back the desires you both had to make things work together. If you find yourself dwelling on this memory, change what happens as you picture it. In your mind, as you both discuss getting back together tell this person that you feel it would not be a wise idea, and that you both need to look out for each other's best interest. Imagine yourself caring for him appropriately and picture him being able to understand and agree. Visualize the two of you peacefully deciding to not pursue the relationship.

Or take another example. Perhaps you recall a time when the two of you were spending together and you became physically intimate. If this memory is presently creating sadness or temptation in your mind, change the event. Imagine the scene transpiring in your mind. As the two of you get closer, imagine yourself pulling away. You tell this guy that you both need to hold off. Then you walk away, calmly and confidently, to the other end of the room or out of the room all together. You picture the two of you knowing that this is the best course of action and that it is worth it. You end the scene feeling strong and at peace.

Re-imagining past events can encourage us emotionally in the right direction. Our mental images hold power over our feelings and if we can mold them to what is true and good, they can influence our feelings towards health.

5. Write down/memorize Scripture
Look for verses that reflect God's faithfulness and intervention, your value and strength. Add anything that reminds you of appropriate thoughts for your situation and anything

that feels empowering. Just as dwelling on your situation influences your heart, so then does focusing on truths. Ask God to show you insightful verses about your particular journey and write down the ones that touch your heart. Maybe carry around a note that has the verse(s) written out. Read them often, memorize a couple at least, and bring them to your mind during the day.

Your spoken voice is an effective tool for you. If you find yourself dwelling and unable to let the thought go, say something aloud. It is often more effective to fight thoughts with words rather than with other thoughts. You may start by saying, "Stop." This grabs the attention of the mind and redirects it. Then you can go on to say a verse of Scripture. Some I like for such a time are:

"...We take captive all thoughts to make them obedient to Christ." (2 Corinthians 10:5)

"Whatever is true, whatever is noble, whatever is right, whatever is pure, whatever is lovely...think about such things." (Philippians 4:8)

"I can do all things through Him who gives me strength." (Philippians 4:13)

Say the verse(s) aloud and really meditate, really absorb each word by saying it slowly.

By focusing on what is good and true, the unhealthy thoughts become naturally replaced. It's like turning the light on in a dark room. When the light is turned on, the darkness just goes. As I said earlier, it is not about focusing on the unhealthy thoughts to alter them, but focusing on good things that will overpower them and take their place.

Releasing Our Thoughts

When the Clarity Comes

Sometimes we reach moments when we just feel mentally stuck. Our thoughts are running through the same ideas in some sort of cycle and we're not getting anywhere. We want some sort of revelation or deeper grasping but it isn't coming. Many times we are trying to figure out what to do, for example, and we keep covering the same ground over and over. We are trying to see something different, more enlightening and helpful, but we aren't getting there.

However, if we are stuck then it is actually from letting go that the answers come more clearly. Often we can be so afraid of releasing our efforts because we think that if we do, nothing will happen. The irony is that we are only increasing the chance that nothing will happen, when our minds are stuck in a pattern. Here we are preventing any new idea from coming in or being seen to begin with. When we are dwelling on the same thoughts over and over expecting to see something different, we will only be left with the same thoughts over and over. As well as completely robbed of any rest.

I am here to tell you good news – you don't have to do this to yourself anymore! The truth is that if this isn't working, you don't have to do it (nor should you). Sometimes what we need most is simply to unclench our gasp and let go. Here we acknowledge that we have been trying to do this ourselves and are willing to put our trust in Someone else. Here we are daring to believe that if we let go, the truth will come back to us. And it is here that clarity comes. When we stop over thinking we have the space to hear from God. Otherwise there can be so much noise that we are simply unable to hear the often quiet, deep leading He provides.

May you intentionally quiet yourself if you feel you are in an obsessive rut. And may you embrace God, asking Him to speak and help you hear. Then He will indeed bring you the new vision Himself, seemingly out of nowhere. It's time we put our trust on Someone who is indeed more powerful than we are.

Putting it all in Perspective

Good news ladies, you don't have to do all of this perfectly. It is not going to ruin your hope if you don't. Also, nothing that happens around you is going to end the world.

Often we can magnify every little thing. This goes for trying to be perfect, or trying to get others to like us, or trying to care for someone, just to name a few. We often have experiences in the past that teach us we can't make mistakes. But we need to realize that we are not where we were and our present life is different. We can be imperfect and still be alright. Things around us can be imperfect and not overwhelm us.

Just because we are naturally inclined to feel something strongly doesn't mean it really is a big deal in reality. It doesn't mean it has a huge impact on our life and future. We got to tell ourselves, "You know what, this is just not that big of a deal!"

I have used this kind of tactic when I feel burdened. Times I was plagued with obsessing over thoughts like, maybe I shouldn't have said that, what is he thinking now, what do I do next? As if every little thing has enormous consequences and anything that has already happened can't ever be changed. Then I think it all has a great weight on my life, since it feels scary and important. I think it affects everything else like, how others see me, how I see myself or what happens from here. These are the times when instead of thinking about it further, I have do be rid of those thoughts and see more logically and more clearly. Simply, I just need to do away with those silly, false fears. I need to stop myself, laugh and say,

"It's really okay." Here we take away the feeling of power in these thoughts and our emotions start to quiet down, while our attachment is not encouraged to grow.

Try it. Say something like this to yourself slowly, while taking it in. It really does bring more freedom to your mind and heart. Give away that "end of the world" feeling that isn't true at all. And let yourself feel freer.

Exercise: Visualize holding your concerns and lifting them up to God. Feel the burdens being lifted off. Let Him quiet your heart. Ask Him to bring what He knows you need.

2. Watching Behavior

I just spent a great deal of time on your thoughts because they affect your heart *and* they affect your actions. If you see things the way God does, you lose the desire for the wrong things you wanted before and then you don't do things that keep the attachment going. It is crucial to use our truth-filled thoughts as a guide for our behavior. After all, our behavior has a huge impact on whether we stay attached or not.

Now, attachment encourages us to treat the person with more importance than others. We want to call him more often than anyone else, share more of our lives with him and talk in such a way as to encourage specific, desired responses. We feel an agitating need to do these things and feel that if completed, we can experience a sense of relief. However, this sort of behavior encourages our feelings of attachment, thereby allowing for more future anxiety.

Like shifting our thoughts, choosing to behave or not behave in a certain way requires conscious determination. We think about what might occur if we took part in a particular action and if it would hurt or help us in the long run. Then we act based on that. If we feel the desire to contact this person, we must carefully consider the option and be prepared to *decide* not to. If we think about going back to the person, we must remember the truth and make the decision that it cannot happen. We put faith in God, knowing that we are not doing this alone. He is close to us and in our situation and He won't let us miss the right thing. He is in fact, leading us to something better.

Of course, giving in to what we feel like doing does feel relieving on the outset. But soon later it confines us to the cycle of deepened attachment. We often feel more anxiety, sensitivity and confusion. It can leave us feeling hurt, angry and/or unfulfilled. On the other hand, while holding back may at first feel agitating and uncomfortable, once the choice has been made and settled in, a deeper peace will fall upon us...one that will last and grow. We end up feeling much better than if we had given in. The hardest part is making the initial move away from a specific, unhealthy action. After getting over that bump the ground does feel smoother.

Behavior builds on itself. If we allow our emotions to dictate what we do in one circumstance, then there is a likely chance it may be too hard to withstand further actions the next time. It is a slippery slope. The first step makes the next few too easy and before you know it you're down the ramp. We think that doing this one thing is safe "enough" and will satisfy our needs. But instead of gratifying the desire for intimacy, giving into attachment kind of behavior only enlarges it. For example, if you give in and call this person, you will then want to call again not long after that. Your urge to see him will return in full force and you feel back where you started. It is always difficult to restrain ourselves initially. But it is much more difficult when we act on our desires and have to try to stop later.

You must be prepared to make an educated decision about how to act as the opportunities present themselves. Again, you always need to ask yourself, *how will I feel afterwards?* Consider the bigger picture, rather than just how you feel in this moment. What you do now is not an isolated event. It impacts how you feel and what you do later.

Also ask yourself, what is best for me? Let me repeat that one...what is *best* for you? This does not mean you choose what is "okay" or "might be alright" for you. We can always rationalize that an action meets those criteria. And we certainly do! However, that is not good enough. In fact, often what could be seen as "okay" by worldly standards isn't even "good" by God's. Choosing the right course of action means taking a breather and doing what is the *best* and *safest* option. This may mean a number of things. It may mean not contacting the person anymore. It may mean not talking about him (or the situation) to your friends, if you notice it doesn't help you afterwards. It certainly may include not going out with him when you find an excuse to. It means paying attention to what feels peaceful through prayer and approaching the situation as God sees it. It means treating the situation appropriately.

For some of you, this will be a withdrawing process. You may have been so involved in this man's life that even pulling away at all feels impossible. Complete letting go may be unfathomable at first, but if you know after careful prayer that that is right for you, then you seriously walk towards it step by step. Others of you will need to make that complete break immediately because otherwise, your attachment will not change. You may need to get as far away from this guy as possible and make a clean sweep in your life. Or it may mean temporarily holding back with a friend, even if that can begin changing later. Ask God and observe what feels most right, peaceful and steady, within you.

While I was holding back with Luke I was tempted to say to myself, "Since we are friends, I can act in whatever friendly way I want." It can be very easy to justify behavior when you are friends with the guy. Realizing this, I attempted to pause and ask myself, "But is this how I would act with a girlfriend of mine?" If the answer was, "Probably not," then it was not appropriate. At the same time, there were occasions when it was good for me to act a certain way with a girlfriend, but not with Luke. I had to be sensitive to handling my friendship with Luke in a way that felt right. And in a way that felt right to me during each moment. Sometimes this meant backing off completely for some time until I felt less emotionally sensitive. We need to pay careful attention to what this time calls for. This brings me to my next point...

It is easy to measure our success with regard to generalities, rather than act according to our *specific, current* circumstances. We say to ourselves, "Well, this person did (fill in the blank), so I can too." Or, "This is how they manage *their* friendship." However, the course of this situation cannot be determined by other people, or even by how we manage other relationships in our lives. This certain scenario needs to be seen and measured by its own unique factors. Our viewpoint and behavior around it should be based only on what God desires for it specifically, and at this time specifically. That is how we need to judge and prepare for all of our decisions... by looking into the details of what is before us and listening for God's leading in our hearts.

Avoiding Certain Conversations

Watch out for the *types* of conversations you share with this guy. Any talks about the romantic relationship and about past, heartfelt events, or a possible future together, are easy traps that maintain attachment and hinder letting go. Sometimes even the mention of such issues is dangerous, because our minds quickly go there and we begin to dwell. In attachment, we wear our hearts on our sleeves. Any bringing up of emotionally laden memories can weigh on our minds and stay there. You will find that if you keep whatever interchanges you have with this person in "friend" or "acquaintance" language, you will begin feeling better by avoiding more emotional hardship.

We should also be cautious to avoid the same conversation traps that always created more annoyance and anger than productive change. If a topic arises that you both have argued about at length in the past, don't pursue it again in hopes there will be a different outcome this time. I know, you want to prove your point. Maybe finally he will get it. You once again feel the need for him to see things the way you do, because in the past he wouldn't budge and instead wanted *you* to change your opinion. But you think that maybe now he'll understand. If this talk is successful maybe we *can* work together, or at least be able to move on. Sound good?

The problem is we often don't get anything different when we go down the same road. And we only become more attached and invested in the other person, in the process.

Let us consider instead, that we have a choice at the onset of such talks. As the topic is brought to memory yet again, we have the choice of either trying to bring it up for the hundredth time, maybe by using a different tactic, or we can face the limitations of these discouraging talks. We can understand that the venture is pointless and only needlessly frustrating. If we listen to what we truly know, chances are we already know how he will respond and it is only a tiny part of us that expects something different.

Of course the desire to be understood and the hope for success are difficult longings to give up. But sometimes, holding on to them and continuing to try is far more difficult than we let ourselves admit. When a path doesn't succeed, pursuing it again only makes us feel worse. And our need to receive something (like understanding or agreement) from the guy only grows. It reminds us of the past, of all our old feelings and it continues the attachment (even if we feel angry).

Let this be a time you approach the event differently. Step back and tell yourself that it is okay for you to just know something yourself. You don't need him to "get it." Your opinion is enough.

We are not defined by another's ability to understand us and agree with our points. We can choose to take a breather and let it go.

In letting go of attachment the key is *letting go*. This kind of relinquishing is a conscious action *to not* reach out in the way you desire to. The power of not pursuing is significant. There is a behavior in "not" behaving that draws the strength away from the attachment by starving it.

What to Do if He Won't Let Go

Perhaps you are in a situation where the guy does not let you move on. You have enough trouble to begin with and he makes it worse by calling all the time, telling you he wants to see you and talking about the future with you. That can be very challenging and unhealthy for you both. I am sorry you have been put in that position.

In this case, you can see holding back not only as something you do for yourself, but also as something you do for his well being. This person may not know he needs his own freedom, but I assure you he does.

Tell him that this pattern needs to stop because it is only hurting you both. Then say that you will hold off for both your sakes. If you have told him that before and he still persists, then you need to refrain from returning his calls, emails, etc. Do this for as long as it takes before he lets go himself. I know this can be very tough, but it is the best thing you can do. He will at least know why you are holding back. I know you may not want to hurt him or for it to end this way. It is unfortunate that he may not be able to see what you can at this point, though he may later. Know that this difficult season will pass, and you will be glad that you did the right thing.

Try to share with a few trusted friends or a counselor. Share with someone who can hold you accountable and will encourage you with truths when you need to hear them. Just remember, you will get through this and it will get better. The long term results are far worth the momentary challenge.

If he asks you if you can still be friends, you can say you don't know yet. But that for now you both need distance. However, if this is someone who needs to be completely out of your life, you can make it clear that any future contact is not good for either of you and it simply won't happen.

Wavering with His Behavior

It is easy for your behavior to waver as a result of his. Maybe this person goes back and forth. Take one kind of example…he begins to act like a new person who wants to treat you wonderfully. He seems to have changed all his bad behavior and then after you have let yourself believe it, he reverts back to the same guy you didn't think you could or should be with. That can very be tough. You couldn't help but hope and now you blame yourself for it because you are let down yet again! Of course this only makes you even angrier with the guy and twice as angry with yourself for falling for it.

There are times when giving the guy a chance to change can be important. But letting wisdom and caution guide us is even more important. It is a good idea to hold back from even considering this relationship until time has shown that it is now a truly good, safe place for your heart. And a place God is specifically leading you to. As I said earlier, God has a specific place for this person in your life. If you are considering being in relationship with him, you must not only see if he has changed to become a better person (if that was needed), but also if God is leading you to be with him in that way.

Sometimes it takes getting to know someone again slowly, while holding back. You may be able to observe at a healthy acquaintance-distance. If it feels impossible to do this and not fall back in, you need to consider some time alone to think and see what happens. But think about reconsidering only if and when it feels wise. Remember, if this is what God wants, He will in fact make it happen. You don't need to obsess over it or think it is up to you to make it work if it should. God won't let you miss what is right if you ask Him for that and surrender.

"And Lead us not into Temptation..." (Matthew 6:13)

It is interesting that this verse in the Lord's Prayer does not say, "Lead us not into *sin*." Isn't that what counts? No, in this verse Jesus seems to be concerned with more than the sinning itself. He is concerned with the road that takes us there. Here Jesus expresses the dangers and seriousness of temptation. He knows that it can easily become an unavoidable entrance to sin and should not be played around with. After all, He knows the severe consequences of sin and wants us as far away from them as possible. Just as a father does not enjoy seeing his daughter come close to touching a fire, so God does not like watching us even come near a hurtful experience.

Before we behave in a certain way it always begins with our thoughts to do so. These tempt us to act. Since they are fueled with emotion, if we stay with these thoughts even for a short time *we can't imagine doing anything else*. Therefore, in the moment you think about calling, writing, or visiting, ask for courage. Then reverse what you imagine...picture *not* calling, writing or seeing him. See yourself sitting wherever you are and imagine not picking up the phone, just sitting there. Just visualize yourself doing something other than calling. This will empower your decision towards what is right and away from what is tempting. Since the thought to pursue is a great temptation, any visualizing you do that supports it will weaken your resolve easily and be too difficult to withstand. So it is important to change the thought right away to drain its power before it grows. Then you are walking away from the temptation itself and guarding yourself from pain.

As discussed earlier, behavior easily builds on itself and takes us down a slippery slope. Temptation grows even stronger when we begin to act on our feelings of neediness. Suddenly, we want to continue in our inappropriate actions and we start feeling weaker, less able to resist. We must be constantly aware of what we are thinking about doing and be determined to stand our ground at the onset.

Anytime you know that if you do a certain thing you will encourage the attachment, you need to stay away from it. For example, if you know that by calling you cannot help but want to see him, or share your heart and world with him, you need to stay away from the phone! There were times I did not feel able to talk to Luke without feeling too sensitive or wanting to share too much. So I purposely did nothing. It wasn't wise to put myself in a position to be overly tempted and then hurt. While staying away from it was hard, it always ended up being far easier to deal with than the times I gave in.

Once again, this works well particularly after deciding what you want. It is after you have made the decision that what you want is freedom that your determination will say "no" to tempting thoughts and "yes" to embracing what you most deeply desire. Remember that the decision to choose what is best for you will happen more than once. You need to be refueled by your will and God's Spirit on a continuous basis.

Be honest with what you know you need. You need to pay attention to the urge to act within you and pause when it arrives. Think before you act. I recall times I thought about reaching out to Luke and because I wanted to call too much, I didn't let myself first stop to consider if it was best (though something in me felt uneasy about it). I chose to ignore the quiet reservations within me and just followed through with quick reasoning. Afterwards, I was rarely glad that I did.

You can pray that God makes what is right feel manageable to you. He has done this with me on more than one occasion.

Journal Exercise: Prayerfully create a list of goals for yourself. What kind of wiser decisions can you make? What are tempting thoughts and actions to stay away from? Reread this list when you need to.

3. Using Self Talk

Self talk is a fancy term for things that we say to ourselves. Throughout the day our mind is constantly working with statements that we make about ourselves and about our interactions with the world. We may say, "I am so proud of myself for…" or "I am a failure most of the time." We may think, "Why can't I get this right?" Or "This is tough, but I can do it." There are countless statements that enter our mind and each one of them is significant.

Despite their possible brief presence, some thoughts recur. These often come from deep beliefs about ourselves and tend to appear in different contexts. They are based on what we have seen in the past, particularly from our earliest memories. And they carry meaning behind them. For example, if you never felt good enough while growing up, there will be times you battle with that same feeling to this day as you face trouble at work and tell yourself, "I fail at every challenge."

Self talk already contains a power since it is based on experiences. However, it continues to carry power in your life because it becomes a self-fulfilling prophecy. If you are telling yourself you are incapable, weak and unworthy, then your actions will fall in line with those traits. If you tell yourself you cannot accomplish this or that, it feels impossible and you easily give up. These thoughts can be unrealistic and often do not match up with our potential. But if they are believed wholeheartedly, then they are acted on and become our reality.

Reaffirm Truth about Yourself

Use your thoughts to remind yourself of who God made you to be. Think about the positives you and others have seen in yourself. We have this horrible habit of focusing on our weaknesses and forgetting all about the wonderful potential we have seen in ourselves. But the more we notice these positive and hope-filled traits, the more they develop. Our strength and beautiful traits we get from God's Spirit are in us. We just need to turn our eyes to see them. As we do, the glory that lay silently within rises to the surface. We have everything we need to live proudly in the Spirit Christ gave us. Our difficulties and even our fears of them are replaced with hope.

Think often about your true self and don't be afraid to believe in her because she is real. Remember the ultimate value you contain in Christ and how uniquely you were created. In times you consider staying in the captivity of attachment say to yourself, "This isn't good for me. I am truly valuable and I am worth more!"

When trying to let go, I needed to reaffirm to myself that I was worth putting first. I needed to prioritize caring for myself since I was always more concerned about the guys in my life. I tried to tell myself that I needed to do this for me. It didn't have to be about what was going on with him or how my actions (or lack there of) would impact him. It had to now be about doing what was right for me to do, for myself. So I focused on what made me feel peaceful and what encouraged my heart on a path towards health. I would say something like, "I need to do this for me. And I finally will."

Encourage Yourself

As you try to change your behavior, use your self talk against discouragement. For example, if you start to feel powerless to avoid an old habit tell yourself, "I can do this. Even if it isn't easy, that's okay. I can manage and it will get easier." Always believe in yourself as God does.

If you have ever thought that you wanted freedom, reaffirm that thought to yourself now. When you are faced with temptation you can say, "No, I have had enough of this and I want to let go. I'm taking care of myself from now on." Or you may say, "You know, I really don't need this... Nope. Not doing it!" There is great power in straightforward statements that remind us to meet our deep needs.

There is always simple, innate power in contemplating truth and voicing it. These statements strengthen, encourage and deliver the gusto we need to shift in the right direction. Practice saying something emphatic immediately as temptation presents itself, then repeating it if necessary. Believe me, it can make a remarkable impact on your abilities to let go.

You can be your greatest encourager. Use your thoughts in a positive way. They can guide you into strength and away from unhealthy behavior. Then don't forget to congratulate yourself when you find success. You know how hard this can be and you deserve some praise!

Be Understanding

When it comes to recognizing our attachment, we need to make an honest assessment of what is occurring. But we also need to be understanding with ourselves. It is not helpful to tell ourselves we keep messing up and can't get it right. Dwelling on the thought, "I'll never be able to do this," can only lessen motivation and lead to helpless frustration, rather than driven movement towards freedom. Your personal doubts and times of discouragement are normal and to be expected.

Tell yourself something like, "This is so tough, but that's okay. It makes sense how I feel." Or "I am so frustrated I did (fill in the blank), but this is just hard for me. It's a process and I will continue to do better." Again, instead of dwelling on what went wrong, turn your attention to what you will now do differently.

Think on your future hope and not on past mistakes. God is patient with you, yet He is perfect. If God is holy and yet He does not judge you, than you do not need to judge yourself. You can accept God's grace and His kindness, and give the same understanding to yourself.

Journal Exercise: Write some motivating sentences that you can look back on in the future. Include statements to encourage you along the right path.

Chapter 11

Process and Prayer

A Process

Everything about reversing old habits is a process. Our decision to let go and our determined efforts to act accordingly, is a powerful starting point for growth. But it will also be something we need to refresh ourselves in. Feelings change and circumstances arise. Memories come to mind and events trigger the heart. After making moves towards detachment we may find times that feel easier than we anticipated. Then there are other times when we are faced with a choice that may feel harder than it felt previously. If we get through it the healthy way, another step towards complete freedom is taken. But if we fall in an old pattern, we still have not lost our prior success.

Our emotions will respond understandably through the journey. There will be moments of sadness. We will feel a sense of grieving a loss. If this pain never occurs within us it could be that we are not really letting go. The exception to this is when we have become numbed to the other person and have been toppled by too many countless negative interactions. There is no joy left and letting go is only relieving. But for many of us, times of pain and sorrow are to be expected.

If we keep our goals toward freedom in sight, even these sad times will be ones in which we feel a deeper, inner joy that we are doing the right thing. They will also pass. They will become less difficult and arise less often. And times of actually *feeling* joyful, at peace and content will be caught at a glimmer, only to increase in depth and consistency. Then your inner self will feel right and good and the right doors have the opportunity to open. Just remember…*you are gaining much more than what you are giving up.*

Now, there will be times for us women, when we are not only fighting with our old tendencies and faced with spiritual battles, but also feeling just plain moody. Bare with yourself in these times, alright? Please don't get frustrated if you feel the same old hardship. While we should challenge ourselves appropriately, we also need to be patient and understanding. Beating ourselves up does nothing good and only brings us into a negative, unproductive cycle. Again, think about what you can do next, not what you've already done. Tell yourself it is just a process – you're still on the up and up. And remember, God sees consistent hope with you. No matter any mistakes along the way or feelings of weakness, He knows all is well.

This always comes down to realigning our thoughts with reality and prioritizing our health. As long as we focus on God and His truths, as well as continue asking for help, we remain on the right path. Remember the truth and keep seeking it. Then you will be succeeding. When you keep in mind the light at the end of the tunnel, and continue to get up and walk towards it, you will in fact find it.

The smallest step you take towards freedom will be felt richly inside of you. While at first it may feel agitating and uncomfortable, when held through it will quickly prove itself to be more manageable than it once looked. It will also feel completely worth it! Like a refreshing breath of air you will take in this new feeling with energy and sustenance. Like getting closer to that light at the end, you will see more clearly and feel greater joy. And it only keeps getting better from there.

Related to Total Transformation

Letting go of attachment is not growth confined only to this area of your life. Rather, it is part of a greater inner transformation that touches on many places of whole life health. God will use this time to transform you in deeper, richer ways than solely with regard to the situation you struggle with. As mentioned earlier, it is not so much about this scenario as it is about you.

The battles we face around attachment: the desire for love, fears around unmet longings, blindness to truth and stubborn hearts toward surrender, are all elements that appear through our Christian journey. Finding the desire to let go and trying to act in response can be incredibly tough because fundamental human struggles have their interplay right here. Attachment is just one area where these spiritual dynamics appear in our physical lives. That being said, when we begin to change in the area of attachment, the rest of our lives will exhibit change as well. We will live as people who are generally wiser in decision making, more disciplined and more at rest in ourselves. If we have relied on God through the process, we will a greater closeness and security in our relationship with Him. We will feel different within. It should encourage you to know that your efforts in detachment have the ability to bless you in many areas of your life.

Consider this time of trial not as a problem, but as an *opportunity*. Here is your opportunity to become aware of negative habits and live out something different. You may have been unaware of all that needs changing in your life.

Now you can face what you need to and move into a more promising future. You can also be made inwardly beautiful in the process. In your attempts to develop understanding and in your efforts to utilize what you learn, you are being grown in wisdom and strength. Simply in trying your best, in getting up again when you start to fall, you are practicing perseverance and becoming refined in the process. Every challenge that we face is only a wonderful opportunity for inner change and future blessing. In the end the struggle will be over and just a memory of the past. But we will be left with even more - benefits that we will take with us the rest of our lives.

Come to God with the request that He teach you and bless you through this, and He certainly will. I have seen noticeable blessings that have come from my pain. In fact, the most difficult times of challenge have created the changes for which I am most touched.

....

Prayer

"I lift my eyes to the hills - where does my help come from? My help comes from the Lord, the Maker of heaven and earth." (Psalm 121:1-2)

This is perhaps my favorite verse in Scripture because it so defines my heart and inner inclinations the past many years. I know that God is what I need at the core of my being. He alone can affect my heart. He alone can comfort my soul. He alone can create positive change, where I am powerless to do so myself.

Though this book is very much about what we can do to let go, the priority and continuous action that must be greater than even our techniques, is relying on God. We need a higher than human power to break our habits and retrain our hearts. When it comes to the complex, burdensome nature of attachment, we need a greater work done inside of us than one we can create ourselves. Any ingrained pattern needs a greater power to break it. Then there are those deeper needs that sometimes cause our weaknesses. Only God can get to the core of us, heal the wounds and set straight the life habits that reside there.

Let me assure you…prayer, particularly focused and persistent prayer, has great power. Jesus said that, *"According to your faith will it be done for you"* (Matthew 9:29). When we go to God, it reflects our faith in Him (even if it feels small at the moment) and our faith as small as a seed can bring about great results.

Yet we must approach it diligently. I have found that my most significant times of change have occurred only after really taking my time in sincere sharing and petitions to God. He can tell what is most important to us by how much time and energy we allot for it. Likewise, the mighty strength of our requests rises to a whole new level when we block out real time to attend only to that particular set of needs. Recognize the importance of change and be determined to seek it with all of your heart.

Gifts We Receive

Comfort

There is nothing like the arms of our Father to embrace us in times of need. There is nothing like the tenderness of His caring heart to soothe our tired souls. Our emotional struggles attack the very core of our beings. We need the encouragement and gracious understanding of a God who is love Himself.

As we've established, there is no one who can understand and feel our battle as God can. His empathy and ability to completely relate in mind and heart, is itself a comforting companion to our lonely experiences. With Him we are not alone. He is there to *know* our heavy chains. But here is an even better part...He is there to take them off.

"Come to me, all who are weary and burdened, and I will give you rest. Take my yoke upon you and learn from me, for I am gentle and humble in heart, and you will find rest for your souls. For my yoke is easy and my burden light."
(Matthew 12:28-30)

Wisdom

As we pray, God delivers us insight and learning. You will begin to see into the depths of a situation, straight through the surface matter and into what counts. Much of what I have written in this book comes from the lessons and revelations of His Spirit. We need God's cleansing power to clear the way through the dense fog. We need to see reality and clear up our distortions.

God knows our pasts, our hearts and everyone around us perfectly. He knows our futures and possibilities. It seems obvious that He would be our most eligible consultant on all matters! Let us then, always consult first and most with our greatest Counselor.

"I will instruct you and teach you in the way you should go; I will counsel you and watch over you." (Psalm 32:8)

Peace

So often peace is what we need most. We must understand that no matter what automatic, bothersome thoughts appear and reappear God is still mightier than they are. His desire and ability to give you peace does not cower in the presence of even the most stubborn anxiety. His power is exponentially greater. After all, He is the workman of our own minds. He knows how to repair our thinking. Thank God, He still is Lord over every part of us. We can invite Him within to calm the storm.

Do not underestimate God's desire for peace in your heart and mind. It is a priority for Him. Jesus could have said he spoke to us for a variety of reasons, but peace is the one He chose:

"I have told you these things so that in me you would have peace. In this world you will have trouble. But take heart! I have overcome the world." (John 16:33).

Desire

We also need God to incline our hearts in the right direction. When He does, we find not only what He desires, but also what we do. He simply reveals what is deep down already there. But we need Him to help us and enlighten our new self in this battle with the old.

Many of us assume that God desires us to push through nagging temptation to do the right thing. We are meant to trudge along and barely get to the other side. However, God does not even ask for us to make it so difficult. He wants to influence our hearts so that the right thing feels good to us and manageable.

"For God did not give us a spirit of timidity, but a spirit of power, of love and of self-discipline." (2 Timothy 1:7)

Strength

God gives us the power to keep going. When our legs feel weary and our mind reverts to old, fearful places, we need someone to come within our very selves and sustain us to persevere. As we shift our attention from looking to ourselves to fixing our eyes on Him, we begin to be inwardly renewed. Our weakness becomes a place on which His strength settles. We need not be afraid of times we feel weak because they can be blessed opportunities to find a greater strength than we could create ourselves. Even if we have to wait to feel this strength from God, it does begin to come.

"He gives strength to the weary, and increases the power of the weak...they will soar on wings like eagles. The will run and not grow weary, they will walk and not grow faint."
(Isaiah 40:29&31)

Hope

Hope particularly, is dear to God's heart. Without a hopeful vision in our sight we have little motivation or ability to move beyond our current circumstances. But with it constantly before us we have the energy to walk bravely towards a new day. Having hope is shifting our eyesight from what is presently in front of us to the good that will later come. It is knowing we will get there. By gazing on our upcoming freedom and relief instead of our current pain, we enable ourselves to already begin feeling what is ahead. We can look beyond the rain, see the sun in the distance and feel its warmth on our skin.

God often encourages us to know we are on the way to something better and tells us it is safe to rely on this fact. The hope He speaks of is real. It is not some illusion or facet of wishful thinking. It is tangible, attainable and leads to real results that we can physically experience. When we have hope in Him, that He will make things change, He will in fact bring it to pass. As long as He is God, there is always hope.

"No one whose hope is in you will ever be put to shame."
(Psalm 25:3)

Lastly, through prayer we receive the most beautiful gift from which all other good things follow: a deepened experience of our intimate relationship with God.

Some tips in prayer:

First of all, remember that God has called you to come before Him, at that very moment. It is truly a privilege that the Creator of the world invites us to speak to Him and ask any number of things from Him. It is even more special that He loves to hear from us. Here are some pointers for what our prayers can include. Some prayers have all of these elements, while others will just have certain ones. The key is not to follow a recipe but to be authentic, and to get these concepts into our hearts so they come out naturally.

- <u>Praise God</u> for His beauty...that despite our weaknesses, His faithfulness and love remains full. Ask Him to show you more of who He is.
- <u>Be unafraid</u> to be open and vulnerable. Say what you are afraid of, what you need and the right desires you wish you had/wanted.
- <u>Ask to be taught</u> by God - for Him to use this time for your good and growth and for His glory.
- <u>Ask for discernment, strength and protection</u> in the battle around you of temptation and confusion.
- <u>Use Scripture</u> in prayer. Verses you relate to and desire to absorb can be spoken back to God and have power since they come from Him.

Visualize getting what you ask for. If you ask for strength, see yourself smiling and looking strong. See it as you make the request.

Don't give up. We are told to persevere in prayer. Keep believing in the love and power of God and know that He *will* answer you.

Lastly, *just be present*. Take a breather. Consider that Love and Gracious Power surround you. Think of breathing in His Spirit with each breath. Imagine Him smiling down at you with adoration. Imagine Him looking at you with empathy if you are struggling. It does not matter how weak you have felt, how long it's been or how guilty you might feel. God's mercy and compassion covers all, His heartfelt patience never tires. He is just delighted when you are there with Him.

You may also want to read a verse written in this chapter. Just read it slowly, absorbing each word into your being. Memorize one that hits home to you and bring it to yourself in future times of silence.

Pay attention to any feelings and senses in our being. Even if we do not hear or sense something specific in those silent moments, they can quiet us. They can remind us of what we are already feeling. And they can prepare us to more clearly hear the voice of God later in the day or some other time soon. Yet they also remind us of what our prayer time is...*time with God.*

The state of our prayer lives is a reflection of the state of our relationship with God in general (as our relationship with God is a reflection of our prayer lives). If we feel close to Him, if we know He loves us enough to listen and is powerful enough to do something, we will pray more and listen better. So if we want to grow in prayer and experience the benefits of it, we must make sure to be strengthening our relationship with Him. We can go about this by reading Scripture, going to church services, talking with other Christians, reading Christian books, etc. Even when we know God well, we must constantly remind ourselves of just how real, loving and powerful He is. We remind ourselves then, that prayer is completely worth it. We must own in our hearts the character of God, knowing that He is in fact listening and able to answer. Only as we absorb these truths will we approach God as we should and receive all that He wants for us.

The Beauty in Stillness

It is important for us to quiet ourselves. In this world it is something that we often have the hardest time doing, but it becomes easier if we practice it. And it is worth our efforts. We can experience more of God in the silence and a deeper part of us can be cultivated to feel Him in a more inner, intimate way.

When we go through emotional experiences, there is so much we are feeling and thinking that it becomes even more crucial for us to become still inside. I would recommend that after a moment of heartfelt prayer where you let it all out, you take some deep breaths and just sit with God. Try to do this on a day when you have enough time to not be rushed, no where to run to the next moment. Try not to think about the time, just make the moment with God your priority.

Sometimes in a moment of hardship, I just look up at God. Of course I know He is everywhere around me and not just "up there," but it just helps me to have somewhere to visually focus. I look up at Him and I sigh. Or I say, "Father." I lift my heart to Him there. I recognize and acknowledge that He knows exactly what I am feeling, why I am feeling it and what I need. He just knows. And He knows with His heart. In that moment He connects with me in a way no one else can.

There are times that I do this little exercise before praying...if I feel that I am overwhelmed with fear and lack of faith, or whatever negative emotion, I first take a breath

and quiet myself. I sit with God and imagine His greatness.
I sit with Him and imagine His empathy. Maybe I will tell
Him that He is a mighty God who can do anything. I thank
Him that He has been hearing my prayers. I think I say all
this more for myself, actually, just to remember what is true
about Him.

Then I am calmed down enough to actually talk *with*
God and not just *at* Him. Often it is our emotions that we
are praying from and of course that is okay. As I've said,
God wants us to spill our hearts out to Him because He is
our father and wants us to share everything. But there are
moments we need to receive some of Him in the praying
process. There are times it has to be about more than venting.
There are times we want to have less of ourselves and more
of Him – for His power to flow through us, His wisdom to
speak out of us. Then we can pray more in line with His will
and more powerfully for others. It is in these moments of
unity with God, that our words are strong and effective. And
God is actually ministering to us simply as we speak them.

When He feels Far off

Dear friends, many of you have experienced times when
you feel you cannot reach God through prayer or when He
feels distant and far off. Some of you feel that the needs that
you long for are not met and it seems pointless and frustrating to look to Him for help. Let me assure you that these
are times we all have in our lives and it doesn't need to stay
this way.

I do not have the specific answers for why God allows us
to not always feel His presence, power or love. Sometimes
it is because we are unwilling to give up what we hold on
to. He waits for us admit to a particular sin in our lives and
be willing for Him to lead us away from it. It is important to
consider if this is the case with you.

Other times it is to teach us waiting and build us in strength. He sees the potential for us to grow in His beauty, to become one with Him in a new way. And often this kind of work can only happen through challenge, waiting and perseverance. I do believe that in those times God looks at us tenderly and cries with us. He restrains Himself from acting for a certain time and not because He likes to. Rather, God holds back His help only because He knows this is for our good and must be done, even if we can't make sense out of it logically. Continue to listen and knock and "the door will be opened" (Matthew 7:7). Sometimes it just takes time. Just remember, He cares *deeply*. And He looks forward to what will come after this empty time – a season of closeness to Him like you've never had before.

There were a few years in my life when I went through the greatest suffering I had ever experienced and when I looked for God I felt nothing. It saddened me deeply. But I continued to press close to Him, leaning fully on Him and believing He was using the hardship to refine me. I sensed that though it seemed like nothing was happening, it was behind the scenes that God was building something greater in me and preparing me for my future. Then He came in a new way. I not only felt Him again, but I felt Him more tangibly and consistently than I ever used to in my life. And I continue to now. In the end I received a unity with God, an inner strength and an equipping for new works in the future.

People have this habit of giving up too easily with God. Remember He is faithful and He rewards those who diligently seek Him. Don't give up and your time *will* come.

In Closing

Dear **Friends,** God is now guiding you on the rest of your wonderful journey with Him. Along the road He will uncover a beauty in you that He has seen since the beginning. Know also, that God has an astounding love for you. When you follow Him, He cannot help but bring you to real and abounding blessings. He is the author of love, and if it is love that you desire than come close to His heart and let Him take you to His incomparable plans. His are the plans worth discovering. His are the life events worth living. God is at essence a dynamic Creator. And He loves to create new out of old, light out of darkness. The road to the light is not always easy. Oftentimes it isn't. But it gets us to a brighter place than we could have imagined and it's worth the path to get there. Wherever you are starting from today, may you stay close to His side and complete the journey to freedom.

"Forget the former things; do not dwell in the past.
See, I am doing a new thing! Now it springs up; do you not perceive it?
I am making a way in the desert and streams in the wasteland."

(Isaiah 43:18)

My Prayer for you...

* Dearest Lord, you know every one of these women in the depths of their being. You know what they have come through, what they feel and where you plan for them to go. You rejoice over them with love. You see in them the bright promise of their real selves and You desire to show them the same thing.

Lord Christ, I thank You for the courage You have given these precious daughters of Yours to move towards freedom. Please come with grace and power upon each situation, making it entirely yours and making it right. Touch each one of these women personally, in a profound way. Shed your light, your transforming love, in their hearts. Come to those deep places, healing any wounds and removing any lies. I thank You for calling them at this moment and for your desire to bring new life and new gifts. Help them believe. Encourage them today with great hope, increased strength and everything you know they need. They belong to you... God bless them.

"Now may the God of peace strengthen and make you what you ought to be and equip you with everything good that you may carry out His will; while He himself works in you and accomplishes that which is pleasing in His sight, through Jesus Christ our Lord."

(Hebrews 13:20)

Epilogue

I never could have imagined that one day I would be writing a book about emotional attachment. Of all people, how could someone who is so lost in the struggle attempt that? I would need to buy a book like that not write it! But God had bigger plans for me. He used the hard times to teach, soften and slowly change my inner self. He showed up in response to my requests and my waiting. He gave me what I needed to know and He led me to share it. He has answered my prayers that everything would turn out for my good and His glory.

> *"In all things, God works for the good of those He loves, who are called according to His purpose."*
> (Romans 8:28)

Of course this has been a process for me. It hasn't been perfect, but it has still been good. I have learned that I don't need perfection because God's grace is enough for me. Yet I have also been surprised at the strength He has given me, time and again.

Today I have freedom from attached feelings and a sense of peace that I had missed for many years. It is simply wonderful to care for Luke and know he cares for me, while not feeling overwhelmed by emotions. God has shown me that if His hand is on a relationship, He blesses it and creates a special place for it. This even goes for the one's that haven't been so smooth along the way. If He is with them in some capacity, something better will come in time.

I also feel close to God and I have felt more of my true self every step of the way. Of course, I don't have it all solved. I am only human and I will only continue to learn more and develop further, as I enter various seasons of my life. I know that in the future I will have more to say of what He is teaching me. And I will have much more to share about new things He has done.

I always used to wonder if there was a stronger and more peaceful woman beneath the weakness I was accustomed to. I let myself believe that there must be. God always intended to uncover beauty in me and He desires and plans to do the same for you.

As I began feeling the change in me during college, I finished the poem I had written a few years prior (chapter 5).

...She is no longer what I strive to reach for,
that girl in the distance.
No longer what I struggle to attain.
For you saw in me someone else
in the distance of the sun - and I did too.
Now I bow my head in tranquil reverie.
I smile gently and laugh a little perhaps. I am strong.
And in my strength I am filled with a peace so lovely,
that I need nothing else.
Yes, I am her. She is so close now,
that I need not reach anywhere else.

CPSIA information can be obtained
at www.ICGtesting.com
Printed in the USA
LVHW040602300519
619542LV00001B/109/P